The ESSEN of

EUROPEAN
HISTORY

1648 to 1789
Bourbon, Baroque
and the Enlightenment

William H. Burnside, Ph.D.

Professor of History
John Brown University
Siloam Springs, Arkansas

Research and Education Association
61 Ethel Road West
Piscataway, New Jersey 08854

THE ESSENTIALS®
OF EUROPEAN HISTORY
1648 to 1789
Bourbon, Baroque and the Enlightenment

Printed in the United States of America

Library of Congress Catalog Card Number 96-68368

International Standard Book Number 0-87891-707-1

•

ESSENTIALS is a registered trademark of
Research & Education Association, Piscataway, New Jersey 08854

What the "Essentials of History" Will Do for You

REA's "Essentials of History" series offers a new approach to the study of history that is different from what has been available previously. Each book in the series has been designed to steer a sensible middle course, by including neither too much nor too little information.

Compared with conventional history outlines, the "Essentials of History" offer far more detail, with fuller explanations and interpretations of historical events and developments. Compared with voluminous historical tomes and textbooks, the "Essentials of History" offer a far more concise, less ponderous overview of each of the periods they cover.

The "Essentials of History" are intended primarily to aid students in studying history, doing homework, writing papers and preparing for exams. The books are organized to provide quick access to information and explanations of the important events, dates, and persons of the period. The books can be used in conjunction with any text. They will save hours of study and preparation time while providing a firm grasp and insightful understanding of the subject matter.

Instructors too will find the "Essentials of History" useful. The books can assist in reviewing or modifying course outlines. They also can assist with preparation of exams, as well as serve as an efficient memory refresher.

In sum, the "Essentials of History" will prove to be handy reference sources at all times.

The authors of the series are respected experts in their fields. They present clear, well-reasoned explanations and interpretations of the complex political, social, cultural, economic and philosophical issues and developments which characterize each era.

In preparing these books REA has made every effort to assure their accuracy and maximum usefulness. We are confident that each book will prove enjoyable and valuable to its user.

Dr. Max Fogiel, Program Director

About the Author

William H. Burnside has taught European history at John Brown University in Siloam Springs, Arkansas since 1969. He received his degrees in history from Trinity University, California State University at Long Beach, and the University of Arkansas in Fayetteville.

Dr. Burnside has traveled in Europe and has published fifteen articles and two books on historical topics. His latest published work is the book *The Honorable Powell Clayton.*

•

CONTENTS

CHAPTER 1

INTERNATIONAL RELATIONS

1.1 HISTORICAL SETTING IN 1648

The Thirty Years' War (1618 – 1648) had just ended, leaving a devastated Germany and Central Europe of some four hundred semi-autonomous states, referred to as "The Empire" (i.e., the Holy Roman Empire of the Middle Ages).

The Bourbon dynasty emerged stronger than the Hapsburgs, who had dominated Europe for a century and a half.

1.2 PEACE OF WESTPHALIA (1648)

The principle that "the religion of the Prince is the religion of the realm" was extended to permit the Reformed faith (Calvinism) in Germany as well as Catholic and Lutheran Churches.

Dutch and Swiss republics were granted formal recognition

as independent powers. Additionally, Sweden, Prussia, and France gained new territory.

1.3   TREATY OF THE PYRENEES (1659)

The war between France and Spain continued for eleven more years until Spain finally ceded to France part of the Spanish Netherlands and territory in northern Spain. A marriage was arranged between Louis XIV, Bourbon king of France, and Maria Theresa, daughter of the Hapsburg king of Spain, Philip IV.

1.4   WAR OF DEVOLUTION (FIRST DUTCH WAR), 1667 – 68

After the death of his father-in-law, Philip IV, Louis XIV claimed the Spanish Netherlands (Belgium) in the name of his wife. The Law of Devolution granted inheritance to the heirs of a first marriage precedent to those of a second marriage. This law applied in private relationships to property rights, but Louis XIV applied it to political sovereignty.

France invaded the Spanish Netherlands with 50,000 troops in 1667 without a declaration of war. As a defensive measure, England, Holland, and Sweden formed the Triple Alliance.

1.4.1   *Treaty of Aix-la-Chapelle* (1668)

France received twelve fortified towns on the border of the Spanish Netherlands, but gave up Franche-Comté (Burgundy). Furthermore, the question of sovereignty over the Spanish Netherlands was deferred.

1.5   SECOND DUTCH WAR (1672 – 78)

Louis XIV sought revenge for Dutch opposition to French annexation of the Spanish Netherlands. As a Catholic king, he also opposed Dutch Calvinism and republicanism.

France disputed the Triple Alliance by signing separate treaties with England (Charles II: Treaty of Dover, 1670) and with Sweden (1672).

In 1672, France invaded southern Holland with 100,000 troops. William III of Orange became head of state and the Dutch opened the dikes to flood the land and saved Holland and the city of Amsterdam from the French. Brandenburg, the Empire, and Spain allied with Holland against France.

At the war's end, the Peace of Nijmegan (1678 – 79) granted Holland all of its territory back while Spain and France exchanged more than a dozen territories.

1.6   INVASION OF THE SPANISH NETHERLANDS (1683)

France occupied Luxemburg and Trier and seized Lorraine while signing a twenty-year truce with the Empire.

The League of Augsburg was formed in 1686 to counteract French power and restore the balance of power. Members were The Empire, Holland, Spain, Sweden, the Palatinate, Saxony, Bavaria, and Savoy.

1.7 WAR OF THE LEAGUE OF AUGSBURG (1688 – 97)

The Glorious Revolution of 1688 brought William III of Orange and his wife, Mary, to the throne of England.

The War of the League of Augsburg opened the long period of Anglo-French rivalry which continued until the defeat of Napoleon in 1815. France fought against the two leading naval powers of the day: Holland and England, and in three theaters of war: on the Rhine, in the Low Countries, and in Italy.

Known in North America as King William's War (1689 – 97), English and French colonials clashed along the New York and New England frontiers.

1.7.1 *Treaty of Ryswick (1697)*

France, England, and Holland agreed to restore captured territories. Fortresses in the Spanish Netherlands were to be garrisoned with Dutch troops as a buffer zone between France and Holland. Additionally, French sovereignty over Alsace and Strasbourg was acknowledged as permanent.

1.8 WAR OF THE SPANISH SUCCESSION (1701 – 13)

Charles II, the last of the Hapsburg kings of Spain, died childless on November 1, 1700.

The king's will named Philip of Anjou, the grandson of Louis XIV and Maria Theresa, to be king of Spain. In 1698 King Charles had named Emperor Leopold's grandson, the seven-year-old Electoral Prince Joseph Ferdinand of Bavaria, as his sole heir. The boy died a few months later and in Octo-

THE SPANISH SUCCESSION (1700)

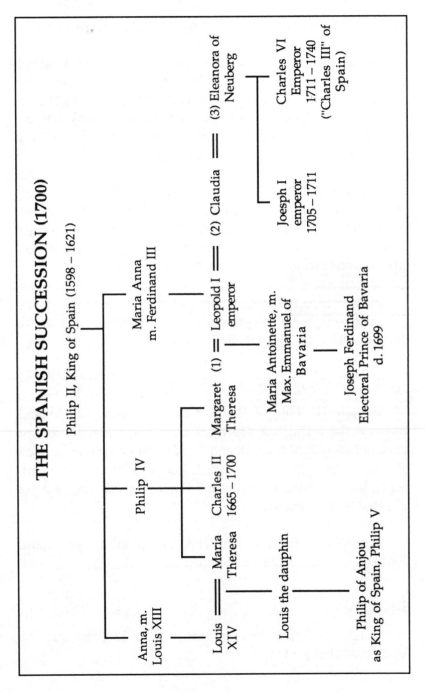

Philip II, King of Spain (1598 – 1621)

Anna, m. Louis XIII

Philip IV

Maria Anna m. Ferdinand III

Louis XIV = Maria Theresa

Charles II 1665 – 1700

Margaret Theresa (1) = Leopold I emperor = (2) Claudia = (3) Eleanora of Neuberg

Louis the dauphin

Maria Antoinette, m. Max. Emmanuel of Bavaria

Joesph I emperor 1705 – 1711

Charles VI Emperor 1711 – 1740 ("Charles III" of Spain)

Philip of Anjou as King of Spain, Philip V

Joseph Ferdinand Electoral Prince of Bavaria d. 1699

ber 1700, and the king signed the new will in favor of Philip.

The Second Partition Treaty, however, signed by England, Holland, and France in May 1700, agreed that the son (later, Emperor Charles VI) of the Austrian Hapsburg Emperor Leopold would become king of Spain and Philip of Anjou would be compensated with Italian territories. (Both the mother and first wife of Leopold were daughters of Spanish kings.)

Issues involved in the War of the Spanish Succession were the future of the Spanish Empire. Additional primary causes were whether the Austrian Hapsburg lands would be separated from Spain and whether the dominant strength of France and the Bourbons would now include Spain.

In a sense, Charles II made war almost inevitable. Louis XIV had to fight for his grandson's claims against those of his enemy and Leopold had to do the same.

1.8.1 The Grand Alliance

William III, king of England and Stadholder of Holland, opposed the Spanish Netherlands falling into French control. England also faced Spanish and French competition in the New World. A merger of the Spanish and French thrones would result in a coalition of Spain and France against England and Holland in the Americas.

In response, England, Holland, The Empire, and Prussia formed the Grand Alliance in September 1701.

1.8.2 War

France and Spain were stronger on land; England and Holland controlled the sea.

The Battle of Blenheim, August 13, 1704, was a brilliant victory for England and the Duke of Marlborough, and one of the key battles of the war. It began a series of military reverses that prevented French domination of Europe.

At the great Battle of Ramillies, May 23, 1706, in four hours Marlborough shattered the French army and held onto the Netherlands.

In September 1709, the bloody Battle of Malplaquet had a contrasting result when the Allies lost 24,000 men and the French lost 12,000.

The allies invaded Spain and replaced Philip with Charles. The French and Spanish, however, rallied and drove the allies from both countries, restoring the Spanish throne to the Bourbons.

The war was known as Queen Anne's War (1702 – 13) in North America. England was faced for the first time with an alliance of its two great rival empires, Spain and France. Though the results there were inconclusive, English colonials were more reliable in fighting than Spanish and French.

1.9   TREATY OF UTRECHT (1713)

This was the most important European treaty since the Peace of Westphalia in 1648.

The Spanish Empire was partitioned and a Bourbon remained on the throne of Spain. Philip V (Philip of Anjou) retained Spain and the Spanish Empire in America. He explicitly renounced his claims to the French throne. The Hapsburg Empire in Central Europe acquired the Spanish Netherlands (Austrian Netherlands thereafter) and territories in Italy.

England took Gibraltar, Minorca, Newfoundland, Hudson's Bay, and Nova Scotia. France retained Alsace and the city of Strasbourg.

As a result, the Hapsburgs became a counterbalance to French power in western Europe, but no longer occupied the Spanish throne.

1.10 WAR OF THE AUSTRIAN SUCCESSION (1740 – 48)

Charles VI died in 1740 and his daughter 23-year-old Maria Theresa (reigned 1740 – 80) inherited the Austrian Hapsburg Empire. Frederick the Great, age 28, (reigned 1740 – 86) had just inherited the Prussian throne from his father, Frederick William I. In 1840 Frederick suddenly invaded the Hapsburg territory of Silesia, and England joined Austria against Prussia, Bavaria, France, and Spain.

Frederick's brilliant military tactics won many victories. His long night marches, sudden flank attacks, and surprise actions contrasted with the usual siege warfare of the time.

The war was known in North America as King George's War (1744 – 48). Colonial militia from Massachusetts captured Louisburg, the fortified French naval base on Cape Breton Island commanding the entrance to the St. Lawrence River and Valley. Louisburg was returned to France after the war in exchange for Madras in India, which the French had captured.

The *Treaty of Aix-la-Chapelle* (1748), ended the war and Prussia emerged as one of the Great Powers. By retaining Silesia, Prussia doubled its population.

1.11 THE SEVEN YEARS' WAR (1756 – 63)

Britain and France renewed hostilities as the French and Indian War (1754 – 63) began at the entrance to the Ohio Valley. At stake was control of the North American continent.

In Europe, Austria sought to regain Silesia with its important textile industry and rich deposits of coal and iron. Maria Theresa persuaded Louis XV to overlook their traditional Bourbon-Hapsburg enmity and aid Austria in a war with Prussia.

Russia, under Czarina Elizabeth (reigned 1741 – 62), joined the alliance. She disliked Frederick the Great intensely and feared Prussian competition in Poland. Great Britain provided Prussia with funds but few troops. Prussia was then faced with fighting almost alone against three major powers of Europe: Austria, France, and Russia. Their combined population was fifteen times that of Prussia.

The Seven Years' War was the hardest fought war in the eighteenth century. In six years Prussia won eight brilliant victories and lost eight others. Berlin was twice captured and partially burned by Russian troops. Still Prussia prevailed. In the process Prussia emerged as one of the Great Powers of Europe and established the reputation of having the best soldiers on the Continent.

William Pitt the Elder led the British to victory. The Royal Navy defeated both the French Atlantic and Mediterranean squadrons in 1759. Britain's trade prospered while French overseas trade dropped to one-sixth its pre-war level. The British captured French posts near Calcutta and Madras in India, and defeated the French in Quebec and Montreal.

In 1762 Elizabeth of Russia died and her successor, Czar Peter III, was a great admirer of Frederick the Great. Though he occupied the Russian throne only from January to July, he took Russia out of the war at a historically decisive moment.

By the *Treaty of Hubertsburg* (1763) Austria recognized Prussian retention of Silesia.

1.11.1 *Treaty of Paris* (1763)

France lost all possessions in North America to Britain. (In 1762 France had ceded to Spain all French claims west of the Mississippi River and New Orleans.) France retained fishing rights off the coast of Newfoundland and Martinique and Guadeloupe, sugar islands in the West Indies. Spain ceded the Floridas to Britain in exchange for the return of Cuba.

1.12 THE AMERICAN WAR FOR INDEPENDENCE AS A EUROPEAN WAR, 1775 – 83

France entered the French-American Alliance of 1778 in an effort to regain lost prestige in Europe and to weaken her British adversary. In 1779 Spain joined France in the war, hoping to recover Gibraltar and the Floridas.

French troops strengthened Washington's forces. The leadership of French field officers such as Lafayette aided in strategic planning. Admiral DeGrasse's French fleet prevented the evacuation of Lord Cornwallis from Yorktown in the final decisive battle of the war in 1781. Rochambeau's and Lafayette's French troops aided Washington at Yorktown.

1.12.1 *Treaty of Paris (1783)*

Britain recognized the independence of the United States of America, and retroceded the Floridas to Spain.

Britain left France no territorial gains by signing a separate and territorially generous treaty with the United States.

CHAPTER 2

ECONOMIC DEVELOPMENTS

2.1 TRADITIONAL ECONOMIC CONDITIONS

Poverty was the norm during the Middle Ages. Infant mortality rate was 50% and sometimes half the surviving children died before reaching adulthood. As late as 1700, the overall life expectancy was 30 years of age.

Subsistence farming was the dominant occupation historically and famine was a regular part of life. One-third of the population of Finland, for example, died in the famine of 1696 – 97. France, one of the richer agricultural lands, experienced eleven general famines in the 17th century and sixteen in the 18th century.

Contagious diseases decimated towns and villages: smallpox, measles, diptheria, typhoid, scarlet fever, bubonic plague, and typhus.

Political and economic freedoms associated with the Protestant Reformation and biblical work ethic gradually began to change the economy of Europe as innovation, hard work, frugality, and entrepreneurship became the norm.

2.2 SOCIETAL INSTITUTIONS NEEDED FOR COMMERCE AND A PROSPEROUS ECONOMY

A prosperous economy needs a moral system as a base for reliance on a complex system of expectations and contracts. This was found both in traditional Catholic morality and in the Protestant Reformation of the 16th century. A modern economy could not function without confidence in people living up to their agreements with a sense of individual responsibility towards the following:

1) Credit

2) Representations as to quality

3) Promises to deliver products or to buy them when produced

4) Agreements to share profits

5) Honoring a bank check or bill of exchange

6) Obligations of contracts – written or verbal.

The legal system in society reinforced individual morality:

1) Legal enforcement of contracts and property claims

2) Bills of exchange and banking (checks)

3) Insurance – and payment of claims

4) Recognition of property rights

5) Avoidance of confiscatory taxation.

Innovations in business arrangements abounded. Joint stock companies enabled enterprises to accumulate capital from many investors. Double entry bookkeeping provided a check on clerical accuracy, enabling managers to detect errors. Banknotes were used as a medium of exchange. The divided European political structure enabled merchants and businessmen to compete as they sought to locate in places with a favorable business climate.

2.3 MERCANTILISM

Basic assumptions of mercantilism were as follows:

1) Wealth is measured in terms of commodities, especially gold and silver, rather than in terms of productivity and income-producing investments.

2) Economic activities should increase the power of the national government in the direction of state controls.

3) Since a favorable balance of trade was important, a nation should purchase as little as possible from nations regarded as enemies. The concept of the mutual advantage of trade was not widely accepted.

4) Colonies existed for the benefit of the mother country, not for any mutual benefit that would be gained by economic development.

The philosophy of mercantilism had mixed results in the economy of Europe. On the one hand, the state encouraged economic growth and expansion. On the other, it tended to stifle entrepreneurship, competition, and innovation through monopolies, trade restrictions, and state regulation of commerce.

As a generalization, taxes were low enough not to discourage economic expansion, since the expectations of government involvement domestically in society were small. There were relatively few administrative officials in a day when communication and transportation were slow and thus did not impede economic activities effectively. Compare France, one of the most bureaucratic states of Europe in the 18th century, with France in the 20th century. Then, 12,000 civil servants meant one bureaucrat for every 1,250 people. Today it is one for every 70 people.

The wars of the 17th and 18th centuries involved dynastic disputes, balance-of-power struggles, and mercantilistic competition for trade, raw materials, and colonies. The economic was involved, but it was not as important a factor as the more traditional power politics of international competition. It would have been less of a factor without some of the philosophical assumptions of mercantilism.

In the 19th century, more thought was directed toward encouraging economic initiative by average citizens to the mutual benefit of the entire country. Adam Smith's *The Wealth of Nations,* published in 1776, led the way to a more *laissez-faire* approach. Smith wrote at the beginning of the American War for Independence:

> "To prohibit a great people ... from making all that they can of every part of their own produce, or from employing their stock and industry in the way that they judge most advantageous to themselves, is a manifest violation of the most sacred rights of mankind."

It was the Dutch and the English who led the way towards

the concept of productivity as a measure of national wealth. As a result, Holland became one of the most productive countries in the world in the 17th century and England in the 18th and 19th centuries. There was always a certain ambivalence, however, in the English attitude, as laws such as the Navigation Acts indicated. Restrictive laws were passed in the early Industrial Revolution.

In France, Jean Baptiste Colbert (1619 – 1683), economic adviser to Louis XIV, used the government to encourage economic productivity and aided in the prosperity of France. But his dictatorial regulations were also counter-productive. For example, he forbade the emigration of skilled French workers and specified in detail methods of production. He also believed that foreign trade was a fixed quantity rather than one that grew with demand and lower prices. France, as most states, had high protective tariffs.

The lowering of interest rates also stimulated investment and productivity. Here England led the way: 1600: 10%; 1625: 8%; 1651: 6%; 1715: 5%; 1757: 3%.

2.4   GROWTH OF TRADE

Expansion of Europe's overseas trade resulted from the discovery of an all-water route to Asia around Africa; the discovery of the Western Hemisphere as an area of settlement and trade; the need for spices for the preservation of foods; and desire for luxury goods from the Far East and the Near East.

Population growth expanded domestic markets far in excess of overseas trade. European population at the beginning of the seventeenth century was 70 million; by the end of the eighteenth century it had doubled. Productivity and economic growth increased even faster during the same period.

Innovative scientific and technological discoveries and inventions stimulated trade. Likewise, three-masted trading vessels lowered the costs of transportation and made possible trading over greater distances. Canal and road building also stimulated trade and productivity.

Capitalist systems of banking, insurance, and investment made possible the accumulation of capital essential to discovery and economic growth.

Urbanization was both a cause and a result of economic growth. Urbanization requires and creates a network of market relationships. Towns whose trade prospered increased in population; towns which did not prosper in trade quickly stagnated. Additionally, urbanization provided the opportunity and market for commercial services such as banking, insurance, warehousing, and commodity trading, as well as medicine, law, government, and churches.

2.5 AGRICULTURAL CHANGES

Feudal/manorial changes began in Europe, especially in England, and were replaced by absentee landlords and by commercial farms. Urbanization, increased population, and improvements in trade stimulated the demand for agricultural products.

The design of farm implements was improved. All-metal plows came into use in England as well as horse-drawn cultivators. Drainage and reclamation of swamp land was expanded. Experiments with crops, seeds, machines, breeds of animals, and fertilizers were systematically attempted.

2.6   IMPROVEMENTS IN TRANSPORTATION

The construction of canals and roads was of fundamental importance (Railroads were not developed until the 1830's).

The canal lock was invented in Italy in the 17th century; Holland then began building canals.

The major rivers of France were linked by canals during the 17th century. England's coastwise shipping made canals less pressing, so it was not until the 18th century that canals were built there.

All-weather roads were constructed after the mid-18th century when John Macadam (1756 – 1836) discovered that a gravelled and raised road-bed could carry vehicles year round.

2.7   INDUSTRIAL TECHNOLOGY

Thomas Necomen in 1706 invented an inefficient steam engine as a pump. James Watt, between 1765 and 1769, improved the design so that the expansive power of hot steam could drive a piston. Later, Watt translated the motion of the piston into rotary motion.

The steam engine became one of the most significant inventions in human history. It was no longer necessary to locate factories on mountain streams where water wheels were used to supply power. Its portability meant that both steamboats and railroad engines could be built to transport goods across continents. Ocean-going vessels were no longer dependent on winds to power them.

At the same time, textile machines revolutionized that industry.

John Kay introduced the flying shuttle in 1733. James Hargreave invented the spinning jenny in 1770. Richard Arkwright perfected the spinning frame in 1769. Samuel Crompton introduced the spinning mule in 1779. Edward Cartwright invented the power loom in 1785.

2.8 FACTORS IN SUSTAINED ECONOMIC GROWTH

Innovation was a key element:

1) Innovation by extension of trade and discovery of new resources

2) Innovation by lowering costs of production

3) Innovation by introducing new products and new ways of doing things

4) Innovation in organizing production and marketing methods

5) Overcoming resistance to innovation.

The development of free enterprise stimulated new ideas. This was made possible where the state was not excessively involved in the economy. In England the Puritan Revolution of the 1640's challenged the royal right to grant monopolies and trade privileges. The English common law afterwards adopted the principle of free enterprise open to all. With free enterprise came the responsibility for risk-taking with the possibilities of losses as well as profits.

Free movement of populations provided necessary labor resources. People "voted with their feet" and found their way to new jobs. Many moved to England from Europe. The population of England in 1700 was about 5.5 million and only 6 million by 1750. The economic growth during the last half of the century increased the population of England to 9 million by 1800, a fifty percent growth in a half century. Because of the Industrial Revolution of the 19th century, this figure doubled to 18 million by 1850.

CHAPTER 3

BEGINNINGS OF MODERN SCIENCE AND AGE OF THE ENLIGHTENMENT

3.1   SCIENTIFIC REVOLUTION

Modern science had its origins in the sixteenth and seventeenth century "Scientific Revolution." "The Enlightenment" was an eighteenth century movement.

Nicholas Copernicus (1473 – 1543) discovered that the earth is but one of many planets revolving around the sun and turning on its own axis to make day and night. He demonstrated that the Greek mathematician, Ptolemy, was mistaken in his idea that the earth was a stationery planet in the center of the universe.

Tycho Brahe (1546 – 1601) a Danish nobleman, built an expensive observatory and systematically pursued Copernicus' theories.

Johann Kepler (1571 – 1630) the first great Protestant scientist and assistant to Brahe, discovered that the orbits of the planets are ellipses which make their orbits in equal times. He explained the speed of the planets in their orbits and found that the planets do not move with the sun as focal point.

Galileo Galilei (1564 – 1642) was Professor of Physics and Military Engineering at the University of Padua. He was the first to use the telescope as a scientific instrument and built a powerful telescope himself.

His discoveries and use of the telescope were a great aid in the voyages of discovery and had a direct effect on navigation. He provided artillery with a means of surveying distant targets for more accurate marksmanship.

Galileo's discoveries in mechanics had far-reaching significance. He proved that all falling bodies descend with equal velocity, regardless of weight. He found that a long pendulum swing takes the same time as the short one, so that some force increases the speed of each swing by equal amounts in equal times.

Francis Bacon (1561 – 1626), Lord Chancellor of England, specified inductive method for scientific experimentation. Inductive observation, the development of hypotheses, experimentation, and organization were to be the keys to scientific inquiry.

Rene Descartes (1596 – 1650) wrote his *Discourse on Method* to build on the scientific method by using deductive analysis on scientific discoveries. He wrote that science must begin with clear and incontrovertible facts and then subdivide each problem into as many parts as necessary, following a step-by-step logical sequence in solving complex problems. Descartes was particularly a leader in mathematics and philosophy.

3.2 SCIENTIFIC SOCIETIES

Scientific societies were organized in many European countries in the 17th century. Italy began the first scientific societies in Naples, Rome, and Florence. The Royal Observatory was established at Greenwich in 1675 and the Royal Society in 1662; private donations and entrance fees from members financed the society. The French Academie des Sciences was founded in 1666. King Frederick I of Brandenburg-Prussia chartered the Berlin Academy of Sciences in 1700. Finally, Peter the Great founded the St. Petersburg Academy of Sciences in 1725.

Sir Isaac Newton (1642 – 1747) taught mathematics at Cambridge, was Master of the Royal Mint in London, and for twenty-five years was the President of the Royal Society. Most of his work was done in astronomy, the dominant science of the seventeenth century. He worked with magnification, prisms, and refraction. He used lenses with different curvature and different kinds of glass. Newton's greatest contribution, however, was in discovering his principle of universal gravitation, which he explained in *Philosophiae Naturalis Principia Mathematica*, published in 1687. He claimed to "subject the phenomena of nature to the laws of mathematics" and saw order and design throughout the entire cosmos.

Science and religion were not in conflict in the seventeenth and eighteenth centuries. Scientists universally believed they were studying and analyzing God's creation, not an autonomous phenomena known as "Nature." There was no attempt, as in the nineteenth and twentieth centuries, to secularize science. "Natural law," they believed was created by God for man's use. A tension between the natural and the supernatural simply did not exist in their world view. The question of the extent of the Creator's involvement directly or indirectly in his Creation was an issue of the eighteenth century but there was universal agreement among scientists and philosophers as to the supernatural origin of the universe.

3.3   THE AGE OF THE ENLIGHTENMENT

For the first time in human history, the eighteenth century saw the appearance of a secular world view to capture the imagination of many intellectuals. In the past some kind of a religious perspective had always been central to western civilization. This was true of the ancient Egyptians, Hebrews, Persians, Greeks, and Romans. It was also true of medieval Catholic Christendom and of the sixteenth century Protestant Reformation. The eighteenth century philosophers, who declared themselves "enlightened," thought that "light" came from man's ability to reason. They rejected the idea that light must come from God, either through the Church (the Catholic position) or the Scriptures (the Protestant position). The Enlightenment opened the door to a secularized anthropocentric universe instead of the traditional theocentric view.

The philosophical starting point for the Enlightenment was the belief in the autonomy of man's intellect apart from God. The most basic assumption was faith in reason rather than faith in revelation. The "Enlightened" claimed for themselves, however, a rationality they were unwilling to concede to their opponents.

The Enlightenment believed in the existence of God as a rational explanation of the universe and its form, but that "god" was a deistic Creator who created the universe and then was no longer involved in its mechanistic operation; this was governed by "natural law." Enlightenment philosophers are sometimes characterized as being either basically *rationalists* or *empiricists*.

24

3.3.1 *Rationalists*

Rationalists stressed *deductive* reasoning or mathematical logic as the basis for their epistemology (source of knowledge). They started with "self-evident truths" or postulates, from which they constructed a coherent and logical system of thought.

Rene Descartes (1596 – 1650) sought a basis for logic and thought he found it in man's ability to think. "I think; therefore, I am" was his most famous statement. That statement cannot be denied without thinking. Therefore, it must be an absolute truth that man can think. His proof depends upon logic alone.

Baruch Spinoza (1632 – 77) developed a rational pantheism in which he equated God and nature. He denied all free will and ended up with an impersonal, mechanical universe – a universe with no one there.

Gottfried Wilhelm Leibniz (1646 – 1716) worked on symbolic logic and calculus, and invented a calculating machine. He, too, had a mechanistic world-and-life view and thought of God as a hypothetical abstraction rather than persona.

3.3.2 *Empiricists*

Empiricists stressed *inductive* observation as the basis for their epistemology, in short, the scientific method. Their emphasis was on sensory experience.

John Locke (1632 – 1704) pioneered in the empiricist approach to knowledge and stressed the importance of environment in human development. He classified knowledge as 1) according to reason; 2) contrary to reason; and 3) above reason. Locke thought reason and revelation were complementary and both from God.

David Hume (1711 – 76) was a Scottish historian and philosopher who began by emphasizing the limitations of human reasoning and later became a dogmatic skeptic.

The people of the Enlightenment believed in absolutes; they were not relativists. They believed in absolute truth, absolute ethics, and absolute natural law. And they believed optimistically that these absolutes were discoverable by man's rationality. It wasn't long, of course, before one rationalist's "absolutes" clashed with another's.

The Enlightenment believed in a *closed system* of the universe in which the supernatural was not involved in human life. This was a sharp contrast to the traditional view of an *open system* in which God, angels, and devils were very much a part of human life on this earth.

3.3.3   *The Philosophes*

The *philosophes* were popularizers of the Enlightenment, not professional philosophers. They were men and women "of letters," such as journalists and teachers. They frequented the salons, cafes, and discussion groups in France. They were cultured, refined, genteel intellectuals who had unbounded confidence in man's ability to improve society through sophistication and rational thought. They had a habit of criticizing everything in their path – including rationalism.

Francois-Marie Arouet (1694 – 1778) better known as Voltaire, was one of the most famous *philosophes*. He attended an upper-class Jesuit school in Paris and became well-known for his unusual wit and irreverence. His sharp tongue and "subversive" poetry led to an eleven-month imprisonment in the Bastille. Voltaire lived in England for several years and greatly admired the freedom in the relatively open English society. He accepted Deism and believed in a finite, limited God who he thought of as the Watchmaker of the universe. Characteristically Voltaire relied on ridicule rather than reason to present his case.

Jean-Jacques Rousseau (1712 – 78) lived in Geneva until he was forced to flee to England because of what the government considered radical ideas. Rousseau thought of man in a simpler state of nature as "the noble savage" and sought to throw off the restraints of civilization. Rousseau saw autonomous freedom as the ultimate good. Later in life he decided that if a person did not want Rousseau's utopian ideas, he would be "forced to be free," an obvious contradiction in terms. Rousseau has been influential in western civilization for over two hundred years with his emphasis on freedom as a Bohemian ideal. His book on education, *Emile* (1762) is still popular, despite the fact that he left his five illegitimate children in an orphanage instead of putting his educational theories to work with his own children.

3.3.4 *Chronology*

The Enlightenment varied in emphasis from country to country; the French Enlightenment was not exactly the same as the English or German Enlightenment. Distinctions can also be made chronologically in the development of Enlightenment thought:

1) The end of the 17th and first half of the 18th century saw a reaction against "enthusiasm," or emotionalism and sought moderation and balance in a context of ordered freedom.

2) From the mid-18th century the Enlightenment moved into a skeptical, almost iconoclastic phase where it was fashionable to deride and tear down.

3) The last three decades of the 18th century were revolutionary, radical, and aggressively dogmatic in defense of various abstractions demanding a revolutionary commitment. "Love of mankind" made it one's duty to crush those who disagreed and thus impeded "progress." In short, the Enlightenment entered a utopian phase that was disastrous when it brought on the French Revolution.

3.4   THE "COUNTER-ENLIGHTENMENT"

The "Counter-Enlightenment" is a comprehensive term of diverse and even disparate groups which disagreed with the fundamental assumptions of the Enlightenment and pointed out its weaknesses. This was not a "movement," but merely a convenient category.

3.4.1   *Theistic Opposition*

German pietism, especially Count von Zinzendorf, 1700 – 60, leader of the Moravian Brethren, taught the need for a spiritual conversion and a religious experience. 18th century Methodism similarly taught the need for spiritual regeneration and a moral life that would demonstrate the reality of the conversion. Methodism was led by an Anglican minister, John Wesley, 1703 – 91. The Great Awakening in the English colonies in America in the 1730's and 1740's, led by Jonathan Edwards, had a similar result.

Roman Catholic Jansenism in France argued against the idea of an uninvolved or impersonal God. Hasidism in Eastern European Jewish communities, especially in the 1730's, stressed a joyous religious ferver in direct communion with God in sharp contrast to Deism, which was at the same time gaining adherents in England.

3.5 PHILOSOPHIC REACTION

Some philosophers questioned the fundamental assumptions of rationalist philosophy.

David Hume (1711 – 76) for example, struck at faith in natural law as well as faith in religion. He insisted that "man can accept as true only those things for which he has the evidence of factual observation." (Then why accept Hume's statement as true?) Since the *philosophes* lacked indisputable evidence for their belief in the existence of natural law, Hume believed in living with a "total suspension of judgment." (But if one must be a dogmatic skeptic, then why not be skeptical about dogmatic skepticism?)

Immanuel Kant (1724 – 1794) separated science and morality into separate branches of knowledge. He said that science could describe the natural phenomena of the material world but could not provide a guide for morality. Kant's "categorical imperative" was an intuitive instinct, implanted by God in conscience. Both the ethical sense and aesthetic appreciation in human beings are beyond the knowledge of science. Reason is a function of the mind and has no content in and of itself.

CHAPTER 4

BOURBON FRANCE

4.1 FRENCH FOREIGN POLICY

France was the dominant European power from 1660 to 1713. Louis XIV, however, was unable to extend French boundaries to the Rhine River – one of his chief objectives.

From 1713 – 1789 no one European power dominated international politics. Instead, the concept of the Balance of Power prevailed. A readjustment of power was necessary in central and eastern Europe as a result of the decline of Sweden, Poland, and the Ottoman Empire. This period was characterized by a power struggle between France and England for colonial supremacy in India and in America.

4.2 FRANCE UNDER LOUIS XIV (1643 – 1715)

Louis XIV was vain, arrogant, and charming to the aristocratic ladies of his court. He was five feet five inches tall and wore shoes with high heels.

The king had great physical endurance for long hours of council meetings and endless ceremonies and entertainments. He seemed indifferent to heat and cold and survived a lifetime of abnormal eating.

Moreover, he aspired to be an absolute ruler with no one challenging his dictatorial powers.

The most significant challenge to royal absolutism in France in the 17th century was a series of three revolts (called *Frondes*, meaning "a child's slingshot") by some of the nobility and judges of the *parlements* or courts of Paris. Competition among the nobility, however, enabled the government to put down the revolts. All three of these occurred when Louis XIV was very young (ages 5 – 11) and made a lasting impression on him; he was determined that no revolt would be successful during his reign.

4.2.1 *Government of France Under Louis XIV*

The king believed in absolute, unquestioned authority. Louis XIV deliberately got his chief ministers from the middle class in order to keep the aristocracy out of government. No members of the royal family or the high aristocracy were admitted to the daily council sessions at Versailles, where the king presided personally over deliberations of his ministers.

Council orders were transmitted to the provinces by *intendants*, who supervised all phases of local administration (especially courts, police, and the collection of taxes). Additionally, Louis XIV nullified the power of French institutions which might challenge his centralized bureaucracy.

Louis XIV never called the Estates-General. His intendants arrested the members of the three provincial estates who criticized royal policy; and the parlements were too intimidated by

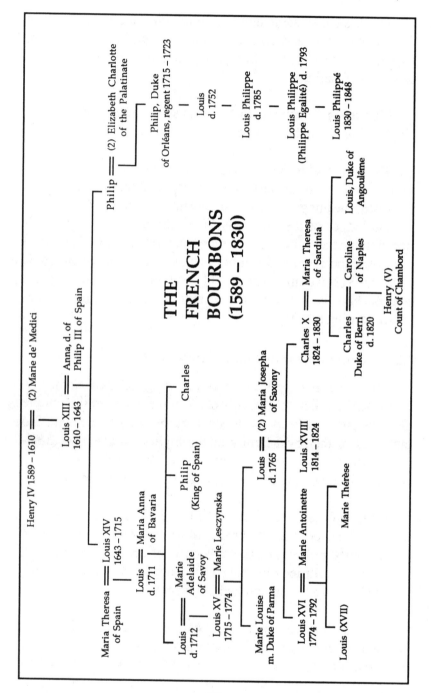

THE FRENCH BOURBONS (1589 – 1830)

Henry IV 1589 – 1610 ══ (2) Marie de' Medici

Louis XIII ══ Anna, d. of Philip III of Spain
1610 – 1643

Philip ══ (2) Elizabeth Charlotte of the Palatinate

Philip, Duke of Orléans, regent 1715 – 1723

Louis d. 1752

Louis Philippe d. 1785

Louis Philippe (Philippe Egalité) d. 1793

Louis Philippé 1830 – 1848

Maria Theresa of Spain ══ Louis XIV 1643 – 1715

Louis ══ Maria Anna of Bavaria
d. 1711

Charles

Philip (King of Spain)

Louis ══ Marie Adelaide of Savoy
d. 1712

Louis XV ══ Marie Lesczynska
1715 – 1774

Louis ══ (2) Maria Josepha of Saxony
d. 1765

Louis XVIII 1814 – 1824

Charles X ══ Maria Theresa of Sardinia
1824 – 1830

Marie Louise m. Duke of Parma

Louis XVI ══ Marie Antoinette
1774 – 1792

Louis (XVII)

Marie Thérèse

Charles ══ Caroline of Naples
Duke of Berri d. 1820

Henry (V) Count of Chambord

Louis, Duke of Angoulême

32

the lack of success of the Frondes to offer further resistance.

Control of the peasants, who numbered 95% of the French population, was accomplished by numerous means. Some peasants kept as little as 20% of their cash crops after paying the landlord, the government, and the Church. Peasants also were subject to the *corvee*, a month's forced labor on the roads. People not at work on the farm were conscripted into the French army or put into workhouses. Finally, rebels were hanged or forced to work as galley slaves.

Colbert, finance minister from 1661 to 1683, improved the economy and the condition of the royal treasury. He reduced the number of tax collectors; reduced local tolls in order to encourage domestic trade; improved France's transportation system with canals and a growing merchant marine; organized a group of French trading companies (the East India Company, the West India Company, the Levant Company and the Company of the North); and paid bounties to ship builders to strengthen trade.

4.2.2 *Palace of Versailles*

Louis XIV moved his royal court from the Louvre in Paris to Versailles, twelve miles outside of Paris. The facade of his palace was a third of a mile long with vast gardens adorned with classical statuary, 1400 fountains, and 1200 orange trees.

In Paris, the court included six hundred people. At Versailles it grew to ten thousand noblemen, officials, and attendants. Sixty percent of the royal tax revenue was spent on Versailles and the upkeep of the court of Louis XIV.

The splendour of the court was in the beautiful gardens and Baroque architecture of the palace, in the luxurious furnishings of the apartments, and in the magnificent dress of men and women who went there. Often half of the income of nobles and their ladies was spent on clothing, furniture, and servants.

Fantastic amusements occupied the time of the aristocratic court: tournaments, hunts, tennis, billiards, boating parties, dinners, dances, ballets, operas, concerts, and theater. In order to celebrate the birth of his son in 1662, the king arranged a ball attended by 15,000 people who danced under a thousand lights before massive mirrors, the Palace of the Carrousel.

4.2.3   Louis XIV's Policies Toward Christianity

Catholics. The king considered himself the head of the French Catholic Church and claimed that the Pope had no temporal authority over the French Church. Louis XIV sided with the Jesuits against the Jansenists, Catholics like Blaise Pascal who reaffirmed St. Augustine's doctrine of inherent depravity, i.e., that man is born by nature a sinner and salvation is only for the elect of God.

Protestants (Huguenots). About a million French citizens were Protestant. Louis XIV attempted to eradicate Protestantism from France by demolishing Huguenot churches and schools, paying cash rewards to Protestants to convert to Catholicism, and by billeting soldiers in homes of those who refused to convert. In 1685 the king revoked the Edict of Nantes that had given many religious freedoms to Protestants at the time of Henry IV. The revocation took away civil rights from Protestants. Their children were required by law to be raised as Catholics. French Protestant clergymen were exiled or sent to the galleys. As many as 200,000 Huguenots fled from France – to England, Holland, and to English colonies in America. Protestantism did survive in France, but was greatly weakened.

4.3 FRANCE UNDER LOUIS XV (1715 – 74)

4.3.1 *Problems and Grievances*

French people of all classes desired greater popular participation in government, rejecting royal absolutism. There was high resentment towards special privileges of the aristocracy. All nobles were exempt from certain taxes. Many were subsidized with regular pensions from the government. The highest offices of government were reserved for aristocrats. Promotions were based on political connections rather than merit. Life at Versailles was wasteful, extravagant, and frivolous.

There was no uniform code of laws, and a lack of justice in the French judicial system existed. The king had arbitrary powers of imprisonment. Government bureaucrats were often petty tyrants, many of them merely serving their own interests. The bureaucracy had become virtually a closed class within itself.

Vestiges of the feudal and manorial systems continued to upset the peasants, particularly when they were taxed excessively in comparison to other segments of society. The *philosophes* gave expression to these grievances and discontent grew.

Louis XV was only five years old when his great-grandfather died. Fifty-nine years later he too died, leaving many of the same problems he had inherited. Corruption and inequity in government were even more pronounced. Ominously, crowds lined the road to St. Denis, the burial place of French kings, and cursed the king's casket just as they had his predecessor.

4.4 FRANCE UNDER LOUIS XVI (1774–1792)

Louis XVI was the grandson of Louis XV. He married

Marie Antoinette (1770), daughter of the Austrian Empress Maria Theresa.

Louis XVI was honest, conscientious, and sought genuine reforms, but he was indecisive and lacking in determination. He antagonized the aristocracy when he sought fiscal reforms.

One of his first acts was to restore to the French *parlements* their judicial powers. When he sought to impose new taxes on the under-taxed aristocracy, the *parlements* refused to register the royal decrees. In 1787 he granted toleration and civil rights to French Huguenots (Protestants).

In 1787 the King summoned the Assembly of the Notables, a group of 144 representatives of the nobility and higher clergy. At Versailles Louis XVI asked them to tax all lands, without regard to privilege of family; to establish provincial assemblies; to allow free trade in grain; and to abolish forced labor on the roads. The Notables refused to accept these reforms and demanded the replacement of certain of the king's ministers.

The climax of the crisis came in 1788 when the king was no longer able to achieve either fiscal reform or new loans. He could not even pay the salaries of government officials. By this time one-half of government revenues went to pay interest on the national debt (at 8%).

For the first time in 175 years the king called for a meeting of the Estates General (1789). When the Estates General formed itself into the National Assembly, the French Revolution was under way. Later in the radical phase of the revolution the National Convention voted 366 to 361 to execute the king, January 21, 1793.

FRENCH ACQUISITIONS, 1660 – 1766

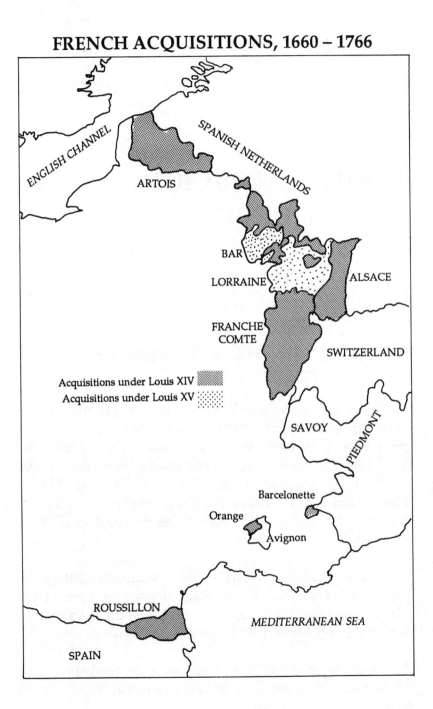

ENGLISH CHANNEL

SPANISH NETHERLANDS

ARTOIS

BAR

LORRAINE

ALSACE

FRANCHE COMTE

SWITZERLAND

Acquisitions under Louis XIV

Acquisitions under Louis XV

SAVOY

PIEDMONT

Barcelonette

Orange

Avignon

MEDITERRANEAN SEA

ROUSSILLON

SPAIN

CHAPTER 5

SPAIN: HAPSBURG AND BOURBON

5.1 SPAIN IN THE SEVENTEENTH CENTURY

The Peace of Westphalia (1648) did not end the war between Spain and France; it continued for eleven more years. In the Treaty of the Pyrenees (1659), Spain ceded to France Artois in the Spanish Netherlands and territory in northern Spain. Marriage was arranged between Louis XIV, Bourbon king of France, and Maria Theresa, Hapsburg daughter of Philip IV, king of Spain. (Louis XIV's mother was the daughter of Philip III of Spain.)

The population of Spain in the seventeenth century declined as Spain continued expelling Moors from Spain, especially from Aragon and Valencia. In 1550 Spain had a population of 7.5 million; by 1660 it was about 5.5 million.

Formerly food-producing lands were deserted. In Castile sheep-raising took the place of food production. Food was imported from Europe. As production declined, inflation increased.

Work was looked upon as a necessary evil, to be avoided when possible. The upper classes preferred a life of cultured ease instead of developing and caring for their estates. Patents of nobility were purchased from the Crown, carrying with them many tax exemptions.

Capitalism was almost non-existent in Spain and savings and investment were below the dignity of the nobility. What industry there was in Spain – silk, woollens, and leatherwork – was declining instead of growing.

Catholic orthodoxy and aristocratic exclusiveness were high values in Spanish society. In 1660, the Spanish clergy numbered 200,000, an average of one for every thirty people.

The Spanish navy had ceased to exist by 1700; there were only eight ships left plus a few borrowed from the Genoese. Most of the soldiers in the Spanish army were foreigners.

5.2 CHARLES II

Charles II (1665 – 1700) the last of the Spanish Hapsburg kings was only four years old when his father, Philip IV, died; his mother Marie Anne of Austria controlled the throne as head of the council of regency. Afflicted with many diseases and of a weak constitution, the king was expected to die long before he did.

He intensely disliked the responsibilities of his office, and his timidity and lack of will power made him one of the worst rulers in Spanish history.

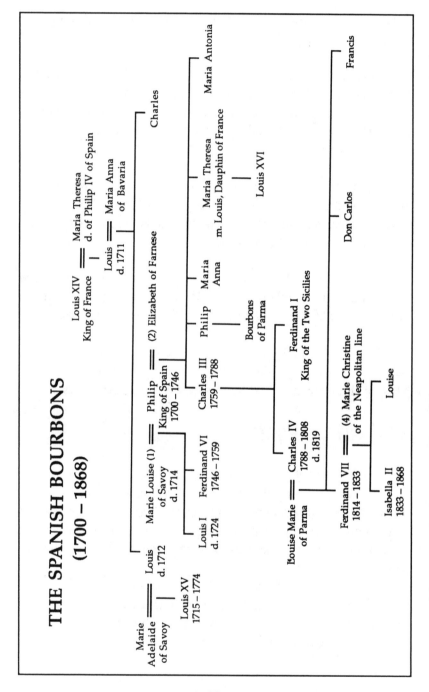

THE SPANISH BOURBONS
(1700 – 1868)

In 1680, he married Marie Louise of France and, on her death in 1689, he married Marie Anne of Bavaria. Since he had no child, Charles II's death in 1700 led to the War of the Spanish Succession (See Chapter 1).

5.3 PHILIP V (1700 – 1746)

The grandson of Louis XIV and the first Bourbon King of Spain was only seventeen years of age when he became king of Spain. The first dozen years of his reign were occupied with the War of the Spanish Succession which ended successfully for him. He modernized the Spanish army and brought it to a strength of 40,000 men.

Philip V centralized the Spanish government by using the Intendant system of the French wherein the governors (or Intendants) of the provinces were under close supervision of the central government under the king. Philip abolished many pensions and government subsidies and restored fiscal health to the Spanish government.

Industry, agriculture, and ship-building were actively encouraged. The Spanish Navy was revived and the fleet was substantial by the end of his reign.

Philip married the fourteen-year-old Marie Louise of Savoy, and when she died in 1714, he married Elizabeth Farnese of Parma. Philip V died during the War of the Austrian Succession and was succeeded by his son by Marie Louise, Ferdinand VI, who ruled for an uneventful thirteen years, 1746 – 59.

5.4 CHARLES III (1759 – 88)

Charles had already had political experience as Duke of Parma and as King of the Two Sicilies. He was an able ruler and enacted many reforms during his long reign. Personally moral, pious, and hard-working, Charles III was one of the most popular of Spanish kings.

Charles helped to stimulate the economy by eliminating laws that restricted internal trade and by reducing tariffs. He encouraged new agricultural settlements and helped establish banks for farmers. He helped to create factories and gave them monopolies: woollens, tapestries, mirrors and glass, silks, porcelain. Schools were established to teach the trades.

By the end of his reign the population of Spain had grown to 10.5 million.

Spain was a strongly Catholic country and Spanish intellectuals were not interested in the doctrines of the Enlightenment, repelled by the irreligion of the *philosophes*. An ambassador wrote in 1789 that in Spain "one finds religion, love for the king, devotion to the law, moderation in the administration, scrupulous respect for the privileges of each province and the individual...."

CHAPTER 6

AUSTRIAN HAPSBURG AND CENTRAL EUROPE

6.1   HISTORY OF THE HAPSBURGS

In 1273 Rudolph of Hapsburg was elected Holy Roman Emperor and gained permanent possession of Austria for the Hapsburg family. The Holy Roman Empire was still intact in the 18th century and consisted of 300 separate states, 51 free towns, and 1,500 free knights, each ruling a tiny state with an average of 300 subjects and an annual income of $500. The largest states of the Empire were the Hapsburg Monarchy, with a population of ten million inside the Empire and twelve million outside; Prussia, with a population of 5.5 million; Bavaria and Saxony, with a population of 2 million each; and Hanover, with a population of 900,000.

The Emperor also claimed authority over seventy-five small principalities.

The custom was to select the ruler of Austria as the Emperor because he alone had sufficient power to enforce Imperial decisions. (A brief exception was Charles VII of Bavaria.) After the War of the Spanish Succession (1701 – 13) and the Treaty of Utrecht (1713), the Spanish throne was occupied by a Bourbon, so Hapsburg power was concentrated in Austria. The Austrian Hapsburgs ruled the Empire: Naples, Sardinia, and Milan in Italy; the Austrian Netherlands (now Belgium); Hungary and Transylvania. Austria was not a national state; its lands included Germans, Hungarians, Czechs, Croats, Italians, Serbs, Rumanians, and others.

6.2 GOVERNMENT OF THE AUSTRIAN EMPIRE

Since different parts of the Empire bore a different legal relationship to the Emperor, there was no single constitutional system or administration for all parts of the realm. The Emperor was duke of Austria, margrave of Styria, duke of Carinthia, Lord of Swabia, count of Tyrol, king of Bohemia, king of Hungary, Transylvania, Croatia, Slavonia and Dalmatia, besides his titles in Italy and the Austrian Netherlands.

The Hapsburg Empire had four chancelleries: the Austrian (with two chancellors); the Bohemian; the Hungarian; and the Translyvanian. There were also departments responsible for the affairs of Italy and the Austrian Netherlands.

In addition the Central Government under the Emperor consisted of the Privy Council (*Geheimer Rat*), which discussed high policy; the *Hofkammer*, which made decisions regarding finance and trade; the *Hofkriegsrat* which was the War Council; the Imperial Chancellery, which dealt with matters of Empire; and the Court Chancellery, which dealt with domestic matters.

THE GERMAN HAPSBURGS (1556 – 1835)

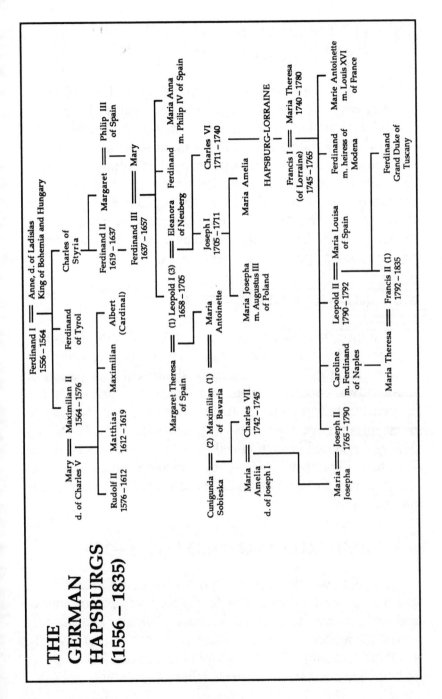

6.3 FEUDALISM IN THE HAPSBURG EMPIRE

The lords of the manor had political as well as economic controls over the peasants. Peasants were under the judicial authority of the lord. They could not marry without the lord's consent. Their children could not work or serve an apprenticeship outside the estate. The peasant could not contract a loan or sell without the lord's consent. Peasants were obligated to the corvée, or compulsory labor, for as many as 100 days a year. Peasants were obliged to buy products supplied by the lord at the prices he set. There were tolls to pay, customs duties, duties on transactions, quit-rents and other taxes.

6.4 MUSIC AND VIENNA

The most famous and popular of the arts in the Hapsburg Empire, and especially in Vienna, was music. Leopold I, a composer himself, was particularly significant as a patron of music. Royal concerts, ballets, and operas were part of the life of Vienna. Italians came to Austria, Bohemia, and Hungary to direct or improve their musical productions. The Slavs and Magyars excelled in singing and playing of instruments. Adam Michna z Otradovic (1600 – 76) composed hymns based on Czech poetry and the famous *St. Wenceslas Mass*, honoring the national hero.

6.5 EMPEROR LEOPOLD I (1658 – 1705)

Leopold I was the first cousin of King Louis XIV of France and also of King Charles II of Spain. He loved poetry, music, and was a patron of the arts. A devout Catholic, Leopold followed the advice of the Jesuits and sought to restrict severely his Protestant subjects. He employed German and Italian artists to build and decorate Baroque churches and palaces.

One of Leopold's most severe tests came with the Turkish invasion of Austria and siege of Vienna itself in 1683. The Turks were driven back by the Poles, Austrians, and Hungarians.

Emperor Leopold was a key figure in the War of Spanish Succession (See Chapter 1).

6.6   EMPEROR CHARLES VI (1711 – 40)

Following a brief reign by his older brother, Joseph I (1705 – 11), who died of smallpox at the age of thirty-three, Charles VI, son of Leopold I, came to the Austrian throne. Charles VI had a keen sense of duty and lived a conscientiously moral life. He was meticulous in his administration and personally involved in the details of governing.

Early in his reign he signed the Treaty of Szatmar with the Hungarians, recognizing their particular liberties and returning the Crown to St. Stephen. The Hungarian Chancellery was to be autonomous within the administration.

6.7   MARIA THERESA (1740 – 80)

Maria Theresa was not really the "Empress" although she was often referred to as such. First her husband and then her son was Emperor of the Holy Roman Empire. Technically she was "Queen of Bohemia and Hungary, Archduchess of Austria, ..." et. al.

Maria Theresa was a beautiful, courageous, high-minded, pious, and capable ruler. Her first reform was to increase the Austrian standing army from 30,000 to 108,000 by persuading the various estates to accept tax reforms and a tax increase. She gradually centralized the Empire and increased the power of the Austrian government.

Maria Theresa was a conservative Catholic, and considered the Church and the nobility to be the foundations of her state. She was concerned, however, with the freedom and well-being of her subjects and political realism was the hallmark of her reign. The two most important international events of her forty-year reign were the War of the Austrian Succession (1740 – 48) and the Seven Years' War (1756 – 63) (See Chapter 1).

6.8   JOSEPH II (1765 – 1790)

Joseph was co-regent with his mother for the last fifteen years of her reign. He sought to be an "enlightened despot" – with emphasis on *despot*. He wanted to govern decisively and forcefully, but rationally with the interests of his subjects in mind – at least as he envisioned them. He sought a full treasury, economy in government, and a strong military force. He sought to emulate the achievements and style of Frederick the Great of Prussia. His mother's adviser, Prince Anton von Kaunitz, provided a timely check on Joseph's ambitions. He wrote to the Emperor: "Despotic governments concern themselves with intimidation and punishment. But in monarchies [we must not forget] how much it is a joy worthy of a noble mind to govern free and thinking beings than to rule vile slaves."

Although the Emperor was a devout Catholic, he expanded the state schools of Austria and granted religious toleration to both Protestants and Jews. Joseph II died at the age of forty-nine, having suffered recent military defeats from the Turks and fearing both the growing power of Russia and revolts in the Austrian Netherlands.

CHAPTER 7

PRUSSIA AND THE HOHENZOLLERNS

7.1 BRANDENBURG-PRUSSIA IN 1648

The Thirty Years' War had devastated Germany. Brandenburg had lost half its population through death, disease, and emigration.

Brandenburg was established by the Emperor Otto I in 950 A.D., and the ruler of Brandenburg was designated as an Elector of the Holy Roman Empire by Emperor Sigismund in 1417. By the time of the Thirty Years' War, despite its central location, Brandenburg was still an insignificant part of the Empire. By marriage, the House of Hohenzollern had also acquired widely-separated parts of the Empire. In the west, Hohenzollerns governed the duchy of Cleves and the counties of Mark and Ravensberg; in the east, they governed the duchy of East Prussia.

The Peace of Westphalia (1648) granted the Elector Eastern Pomerania, three tiny bishoprics and the archbishopric of

Magdeburg. Nothing in these possessions showed any promise of those disparate territories becoming a Great Power of Europe. Each province had its own Estates, representing the towns and the nobility. They had little in common and no common administration. The terrain had no natural frontiers for defense and was not economically significant. Its population was sparse, its soil poor and sandy. It was cut off from the sea and was not on any of the trade routes of Europe.

7.2   FREDERICK WILLIAM (1640 – 88)

During his half-century reign the "Great Elector" established Prussia as a Great Power and laid the foundation for the future unification of Germany in the nineteenth century. He took the title "King of Prussia" since East Prussia lay outside the boundaries of the Holy Roman empire and thus was under no oversight whatever from the Austrian Hapsburgs.

Frederick William was the nephew of King Gustavus Adolphus of Sweden and his wife was the granddaughter of William the Silent, hero of Dutch Independence. He sought to emulate the government organization of the Swedes and the economic policies of the Dutch.

Frederick had been well-educated and spoke five languages. He was a strict Calvinist and settled 20,000 Huguenot refugees on his estates. He granted toleration, however, to both Catholics and Jews.

He encouraged industry and trade and brought in foreign craftsmen and Dutch farmers. In each province he established a local government, headed by a Governor and Chancellor, but with control from the central government in Berlin.

His most historically-significant innovation was the building of a strong standing army. He was able to do this only through heavy taxes, a rate of taxation twice as heavy as French taxation during the height of Louis XIV's power. But the Prussian nobility were not exempt from those heavy taxes, as were the French aristocracy.

The Elector sought to encourage industry and trade, but he was in danger of taxing it out of existence. New industries were started: woollens, cottons, linen, velvet, lace, silk, soap, paper, and iron products. One of his achievements was the Frederick William Canal through Berlin which linked the Elbe and Oder rivers and enabled canal traffic from Breslau and Hamburg to Berlin. He was the only Hohenzollern to be interested in overseas trade before Kaiser William II. But without ports and naval experience, the effort collapsed.

The central dynamic of Frederick William's life was his Calvinism, through which he was convinced of the direct protection and guidance from God in all he did. He highly valued learning and founded the University of Pufendorf and the Berlin Library. He was greatly alarmed at the threat to Protestantism implied in Louis XIV's revocation of the Edict of Nantes in 1685 and joined the League of Augsburg in 1686.

7.3 FREDERICK I (1688 – 1713)

The Great Elector's son (i.e., Elector Frederick III and King Frederick I) was a weak and somewhat deformed man, but won the affection of his people as did no other Hohenzollern. He loved the splendor of the monarchy and elaborate ceremony. He built beautiful palaces and provided splendid uniforms of white satin edged with gold lace for his guards. Dinner was announced by twenty-four trumpeters. An orchestra played and the servants wore blue trimmed with gold lace.

Potsdam had been built by the Great Elector. Frederick I built a new palace in Berlin and Charlottenburg for his Queen, Sophie Charlotte, who joined her husband in the many philosophical and religious discussions common in the palace.

Frederick I founded the University of Halle in 1692, a center for two of the great concepts of the time, Pietism and Natural Law. The king welcomed as immigrants not only craftsmen, but also scholars such as Jacob Lenfant, historian of the Council of Trent, Isaac De Beausobre, translator of the New Testament, and Philip Speuer, a leading Pietist of his day. The Enlightenment philosopher Gottfried Wilhelm Leibnitz persuaded Frederick to found an Academy of Science.

Much of Frederick I's reign was spent at war, for Prussia participated in the War of the League of Augsburg (1688 – 97) and the War of the Spanish Succession (1701 – 13) (See Chapter 1). Prussia did not gain territorially, but perpetuated the military tradition that was beginning. The costs of war were a heavy financial burden to the small state.

7.4   FREDERICK WILLIAM I (1713 – 40)

This king was quite different from his father. He cut the number of court officials drastically, not only for economy, but because he was impatient with ceremony.

He believed Prussia needed a strong standing army and a plentiful treasury and he proceeded to acquire both. Prussia's army grew from 45,000 to 80,000 during his reign, despite a population of only 2.5 million. 80% of state revenues went for military expenditures, compared with 60% in France and 50% in Austria. On the other hand, he only spent 2% of tax revenues to maintain his court, compared with 6% in Austria under Maria Theresa. Frederick built the fourth largest army in Europe, paid off all state debts, and left his successor a surplus of ten million thaler.

Prussia maintained a large standing army in order to avoid war if possible, a policy that was maintained during Frederick William's reign. The only time he went to war was when Charles XII of Sweden occupied Stalsund. Prussia immediately attacked and forced Sweden out of Stralsund. In 1720 Sweden agreed to the Prussian annexation of the port of Stettin and Pomeranian territory west of the river Oder.

Prussia continued close relations with Holland and with England. King George I of England was Frederick William's uncle and father-in-law. His mother was George I's sister and his wife was George's daughter.

Prussia developed the most efficient bureaucracy in Europe. In 1723 the king established a General Directory of four departments, each responsible for certain provinces. Taxes were high, but income from the royal estates (about one-third of the kingdom) largely paid for the army. The king made policy decisions and left it to the bureaucracy to work out the details.

Subordinate to the General Directory were the seventeen provincial chambers. Merit promotions rewarded efficiency and diligence. The civil bureaucracy as well as the military were based on the principle of absolute obedience and discipline.

For oversight every provincial chamber included a special royal agent, or *fiscal*, to keep a close watch on how well the will of the king was followed. The king also required secret reports annually on all bureaucrats.

The whole Prussian bureaucracy consisted of only 14,000 poorly-paid civil servants (about 1/10th the proportionate number commonly found in 20th century European nations).

The king was a ceaseless worker and expected the same from those about him, including his son, the future Frederick the Great. The king entrusted his son's early education to his old governess, Mademoiselle de Rocoulles, a Huguenot refugee who taught Frederick to speak French better than German. The king regimented his son's education from 6:00 a.m. to 10:30 p.m. and the young boy learned all the fifty-four movements of the Prussian drill before he was five years old. Frederick William established a thousand schools for peasant children.

7.5 FREDERICK THE GREAT (FREDERICK II: 1740 – 86)

Frederick the Great inherited his throne at age 28. His father left him a prosperous economy, a full treasury, an income of seven million thalers, and an army of 80,000. Unlike his father, Frederick loved French literature, poetry, and music. He played the flute and wrote poetry all his life.

Frederick's philosophy of government soon became apparent. He wrote in 1740: "Machiavelli maintains that, in this wicked and degenerate world, it is certain ruin to be strictly honest. For my part, I affirm that, in order to be safe, it is necessary to be virtuous. Men are commonly neither wholly good nor wholly bad, but both good and bad ...." The king did not believe the state existed for the gratification of the ruler, but the ruler for the state: he must regard himself as "the first servant of the state." All his life Frederick continued to ponder questions of religion, morality, and power. French literature dominated his reading.

In October 1740, the Emperor Charles VI died and in December Frederick ordered a sudden attack on Silesia. Thus began twenty-three years of warfare where the Great Powers of

THE PARTITIONS OF POLAND

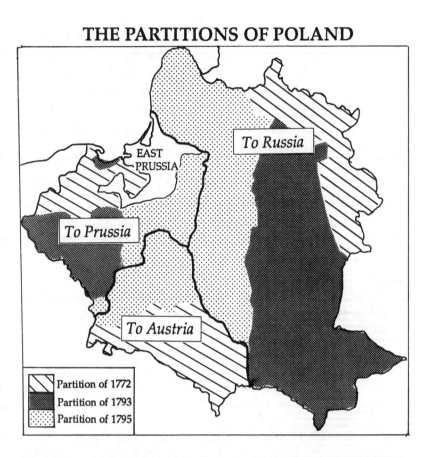

To Russia

EAST PRUSSIA

To Prussia

To Austria

Partition of 1772
Partition of 1793
Partition of 1795

Europe were aligned against Prussia: France, Austria, and Russia. Their combined population was fifteen times that of Prussia. Prussia emerged a quarter century later with enlarged territories of rich land and nearly twice its former population, but at a cost of devastation. Prussia alone lost 180,000 killed and the entire society was seriously disrupted. Indeed, for a time, Frederick thought he would not survive "the ruin of the Fatherland." Instead, Prussia emerged as one of the Great Powers of Europe.

The remaining twenty-three years of the king's life were spent in re-building and reforming what he had very nearly destroyed. Frugality, discipline, and hard work despite very high taxation were the values stressed throughout the society. The king provided funds to rebuild towns and villages, used reserve grain for seed-planting, and requisitioned horses for farming. He suspended taxes in some areas for six months as an economic stimulant. He started many new industries. By 1773, 264 new factories had been built: sugar refineries, leather works, porcelain manufacturing, tobacco works, and so forth. The government drained marshes along the rivers and settled hundreds of families in colonizing former wastelands. He oversaw the reform of the judicial system in an attempt to produce a more equitable nation governed by law. His system was one of "constitutional absolutism."

In 1772, as part of the First Partition of Poland, Prussia acquired west Prussia thus linking most of its territories.

CHAPTER 8

THE DUTCH REPUBLIC

8.1   HISTORICAL BACKGROUND

The Netherlands (known today as Holland and Belgium) were governed by the Spanish Hapsburgs, but each of the seventeen provinces had its own special privileges and limited autonomy within the Spanish Empire.

During the Protestant Reformation of the sixteenth century, large numbers of Dutch were converted to Calvinism ("Reformed" Churches), especially in the North. Catholicism remained stronger in the South (now Belgium).

When Philip II, king of Spain, began demonstrating his determination to use the Spanish Inquisition to enforce laws against "heresy," the Netherlands began to revolt against Spain which continued intermittently for eighty years (1568 – 1648).

In 1578, the Duke of Parma restored many of the old privileges of self-government to the ten southern provinces and large numbers of Calvinists moved north. In 1581 the seven northern Dutch provinces, under the leadership of William the

Silent, declared themselves independent of Spain. In 1588 the great Spanish Armada sent to defeat both the English and the Dutch was partially destroyed by a storm and then defeated by the English seadogs.

In 1648 the Peace of Westphalia recognized the independence of the Republic of the United Provinces. This had already been conceded by Spain in the Treaty of Munster, January 20, 1648.

8.2   GOVERNMENT OF THE NETHERLANDS

The Dutch republic consisted of the seven northern provinces of Zeeland, Utrecht, Holland, Gelderland, Overijssel, Groningen, and Friesland. Holland was the wealthiest and most powerful. Each province and each city was autonomous.

National problems were governed by the States General which consisted of delegates from the provinces which could act only on the instructions of the provincial assemblies. Each province had a Stadholder, or governor, who was under the authority and instructions of the assembly. In times of crisis the provinces would sometimes choose the same Stadholder, and he thereby became the national leader.

8.3   DUTCH ECONOMY

The seventeenth century was the Golden Age of the Dutch. Not only was it the Age of Rembrandt and other great Dutch painters, but the Netherlands was the most prosperous part of Europe in the seventeenth century. It was also the freest. The Dutch did not have government controls and monopolies to impede their freedom of enterprise. As a result they became by

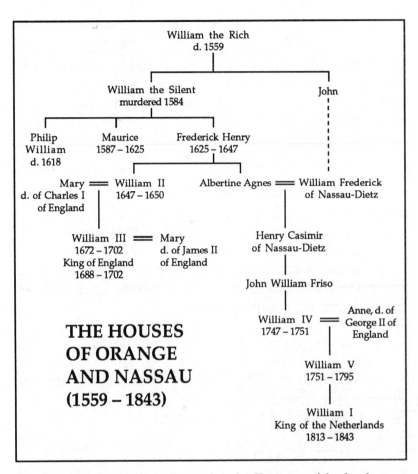

William the Rich
d. 1559

William the Silent
murdered 1584

John

Philip
William
d. 1618

Maurice
1587 – 1625

Frederick Henry
1625 – 1647

Mary === William II
d. of Charles I   1647 – 1650
of England

Albertine Agnes === William Frederick
of Nassau-Dietz

William III === Mary
1672 – 1702   d. of James II
King of England   of England
1688 – 1702

Henry Casimir
of Nassau-Dietz

John William Friso

**THE HOUSES
OF ORANGE
AND NASSAU
(1559 – 1843)**

William IV === Anne, d. of
1747 – 1751   George II of
England

William V
1751 – 1795

William I
King of the Netherlands
1813 – 1843

far the greatest mercantile nation in Europe with the largest merchant marine in the world.

Medium-sized cities and ports were characteristic of the Netherlands: Leyden, Haarlem, Gouda, Delft, and Utrecht, from 20,000 to 40,000. Amsterdam was the richest city in Europe with a population of 100,000. The quays and wharves of these Dutch cities were stocked with Baltic grain, English woollens, silks and spices from India, sugar from the Caribbean, salted herring, and coal.

The Dutch had almost no natural resources, but built their economy around the carrying trade, mercantile businesses, and other service occupations. They were skilled in finishing raw materials. Coarse linens from Germany were bleached and finished into fine textiles. Furniture making, fine woollen goods, sugar refining, tobacco cutting, brewing, pottery, glass, printing, paper making, armament manufacturing, and shipbuilding were all crafts in which the Dutch excelled.

The Dutch taught accounting methods, provided banks and rational legal methods for settling disputes. Their low interest rate was a key to economic growth: 3%, half of the normal rate in England. The Dutch were discussed and written about all over Europe as champions of free enterprise and individual rights – in contrast to state absolutism, economic nationalism, mercantilism, and protective tariffs.

The Dutch East India Company and the Dutch West India Company were organized as cooperative ventures of private enterprise and the state. The various provinces contributed part of the capital for these ventures and the Companies were subject to the authority of the States General.

8.4   DUTCH ART

The 17th century was the most significant in history for Dutch painting. Most of the Dutch painters came from the province of Holland. Rembrandt and Jan Steen were from Leyden; Cuyp came from Dordrecht; Van Goyen from the Hague; and Vermeer from Delft.

The artistic center of the Netherlands was Amsterdam where the Dutch school of painters was noted for their landscape and portrait painting, but especially for "genre painting" in which scenes of everyday life predominate. The Calvinist influence in Holland is reflected in their celebration, but not idealization, of God's Creation. The realistic portrait paintings show mankind as great and noble, but flawed, or, as the Reformed Churches put it, "fallen creatures in a fallen world." Nevertheless, the flawed creation was still to be enjoyed and their pictures of Dutch life in the 17th century show it to be intensely joyful and satisfying in human relationships.

The Dutch painters were masters of light and shadow as were the later French Impressionists. They captured the subtlety and realism of an ordinary scene under the vast expanse of the sky; a storm at sea; or a rain shower "drifting across a distant landscape pursued by sunshine." It is an interesting comparison to contrast the equally-great Flemish contemporary school in the Spanish Netherlands strongly influenced by the counter-Reformation Baroque. Peter Paul Rubens from Antwerp is a good example.

8.5   DUTCH WARS AND FOREIGN POLICY

The Peace of Westphalia (1648) ended eighty years of war between Spain and the Netherlands and resulted in independence for the Dutch Republic and continued Hapsburg rule of the Spanish Netherlands. After being freed from Spanish domination the Dutch were faced with a series of wars against England over trading rights and colonial competition. Then, Louis XIV's efforts to move into the Low Countries brought the Dutch into a drawn-out war with France.

The accession of William and Mary to the throne of England in 1688 brought an end to the warfare between the Dutch and English. In the War of the Spanish Succession, 1701 – 13, England and Holland fought against France and Spain.

CHAPTER 9

ENGLAND, SCOTLAND AND IRELAND

9.1 ENGLISH CIVIL WAR (1642 – 49)

One of the underlying issues in the conflict was the constitutional issue of the relationship between king and parliament. (Could the king govern without the consent of Parliament or go against the wishes of Parliament?). In short, the question was whether England was to have a limited, constitutional monarchy or an absolute monarchy as in France and Prussia.

The theological issue focused on the form of church government England was to have – whether it would follow the established Church of England's hierarchical, episcopal form of church government, or acquire a presbyterian form?

The episcopal form meant that the king, the Archbishop of Canterbury, and the bishops of the church would determine policy, theology, and the form of worship and service. The presbyterian form of polity allowed for more freedom of conscience and dissent among church members. Each congregation would have a voice in the life of the church and a regional group of ministers, or, "presbytery," would attempt to insure "doctrinal purity."

The political implications for representative democracy were present in both issues. That is why most Presbyterians, Puritans, and Congregationalists sided with Parliament and most Anglicans and Catholics sided with the king.

9.1.1 *Charles I* (1625 – 49)

Charles I inherited both the English and Scottish thrones at the death of his father, James I. He claimed a "divine right" theory of absolute authority for himself as king and sought to rule without Parliament. That rule also meant control of the Church of England.

The king demanded more money from Parliament. Parliament refused and began impeachment proceedings against the king's chief minister, the duke of Buckingham, who was later assassinated in 1628. Charles then levied a forced "loan" on many of the wealthier citizens of England and imprisoned seventy-six English gentlemen who refused to contribute. Sir Randolph Crew, Chief Justice of the King's Bench, was dismissed from office for refusing to declare those "loans" legal. Five of the imprisoned men applied for writs of habeas corpus, asking whether the refusal to lend money to the king was a legal cause for imprisonment. The court returned them to jail without comment.

By 1628 both houses of Parliament – Lords and Commons alike – united in opposition to the king.

9.1.2 *The Petition of Right* (1628)

The Parliament in effect bribed the king by granting him a tax grant in exchange for his agreement to the Petition of Right.

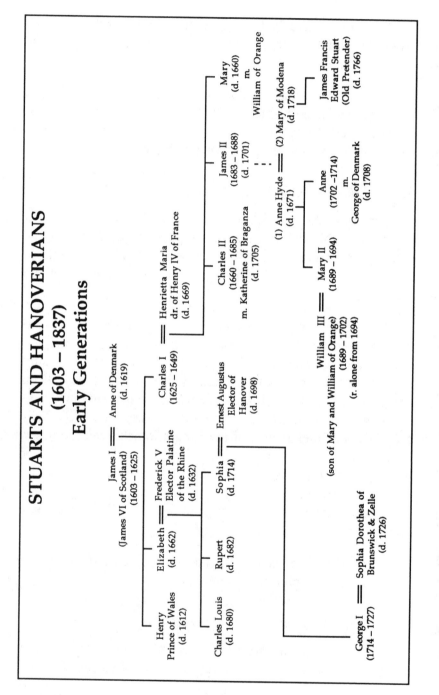

STUARTS AND HANOVERIANS
(1603 – 1837)
Early Generations

James I
(James VI of Scotland)
(1603 – 1625)
═══ Anne of Denmark
(d. 1619)

Henry
Prince of Wales
(d. 1612)

Elizabeth
(d. 1662)
═══ Frederick V
Elector Palatine
of the Rhine
(d. 1632)

Charles Louis
(d. 1680)

Rupert
(d. 1682)

Sophia
(d. 1714)
═══ Ernest Augustus
Elector of
Hanover
(d. 1698)

Charles I
(1625 – 1649)
═══ Henrietta Maria
dr. of Henry IV of France
(d. 1669)

Charles II
(1660 – 1685)
m. Katherine of Braganza
(d. 1705)

James II
(1683 – 1688)
(d. 1701)
(1) Anne Hyde
(d. 1671)
═══ ═ ═ ═ (2) Mary of Modena
(d. 1718)

Mary
(d. 1660)
m.
William of Orange

James Francis
Edward Stuart
(Old Pretender)
(d. 1766)

William III
(son of Mary and William of Orange)
(1689 – 1702)
(r. alone from 1694)
═══ Mary II
(1689 – 1694)

Anne
(1702 –1714)
m.
George of Denmark
(d. 1708)

George I
(1714 – 1727)
═══ Sophia Dorothea of
Brunswick & Zelle
(d. 1726)

64

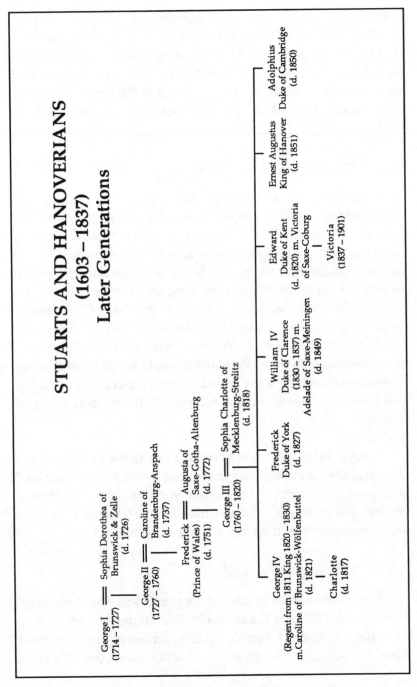

STUARTS AND HANOVERIANS
(1603 – 1837)
Later Generations

George I (1714 – 1727?) ══ Sophia Dorothea of Brunswick & Zelle (d. 1726)

George II (1727 – 1760) ══ Caroline of Brandenburg-Anspach (d. 1737)

Frederick (Prince of Wales) (d. 1751) ══ Augusta of Saxe-Gotha-Altenburg (d. 1772)

George III (1760 – 1820) ══ Sophia Charlotte of Mecklenburg-Strelitz (d. 1818)

George IV (Regent from 1811 King 1820 – 1830) m.Caroline of Brunswick-Wölfenbuttel (d. 1821)

Charlotte (d. 1817)

Frederick Duke of York (d. 1827)

William IV Duke of Clarence (1830 – 1837) m. Adelade of Saxe-Meiningen (d. 1849)

Edward Duke of Kent (d. 1820) m. Victoria of Saxe-Coburg

Victoria (1837 – 1901)

Ernest Augustus King of Hanover (d. 1851)

Adolphius Duke of Cambridge (d. 1850)

It stipulated that no one should pay any tax, gift, loan, or contribution except as provided by Act of Parliament; no one should be imprisoned or detained without due process of law; all were to have the right to the writ of habeas corpus; there should be no forced billeting of soldiers in the homes of private citizens; and that martial law was not to be declared in England.

9.1.3   *The Parliament of 1629*

In the midst of a stormy debate over theology, taxes, and civil liberties, the king sought to force the adjournment of Parliament. But when he sent a message to the Speaker ordering him to adjourn, some of the more athletic members held him in his chair while the door of the House of Commons was locked to prevent the entry of other messengers from the king. (That famous date was March 2, 1629.) A number of resolutions passed. Innovations towards Catholicism or Arminianism were to be regarded as treason. Whoever advised any collection of taxes without consent of Parliament would be guilty of treason. Whoever should pay a tax levied without the consent of Parliament would be considered a betrayer of liberty and guilty of treason.

A royal messenger was allowed to enter the Commons and declared the Commons adjourned and a week later Charles I dissolved Parliament – for eleven years, 1629 – 40. Puritan leaders and leaders of the opposition in the House of Commons were imprisoned by the king, some for several years.

9.1.4   *Religious Persecution*

The established Church of England was the only legal church under Charles I, a Catholic. Within the Church of England (i.e., Anglican Church), specific ministers might be more Catholic, Arminian Protestant, or Puritan (with both Calvinist and Lutheran emphases.)

Conventicles were harshly suppressed. (Conventicles were secret meetings for worship in which the authorized Prayer Book was not used, but the Bible and the Psalter were.)

William Laud, Archbishop of Canterbury, sought to enforce the king's policies vigorously. Arminian clergymen were to be tolerated, but Puritan clergymen silenced. Criticism was brutally suppressed. No book or pamphlet could legally be printed or sold without a license. Puritans who wrote secret pamphlets were punished harshly: In 1630 Alexander Leighton was whipped, pilloried, and mutilated for printing *An Appeal to Parliament* in which he challenged episcopacy. Three others had their ears cut off; one was branded on the cheek with the letters, *SL* (Seditious Libeler). Several were executed.

9.1.5 *National Covenant of Scotland* (1638)

Dissatisfaction with royal absolutism reached a crisis in Scotland when representatives of the Scottish people met at Greyfriars Kirk in Edinburgh in 1638 to sign a national protest against the policies of King Charles, who was king of Scotland as well as King of England. The nobility and barons met and signed the National Covenant one day and the burgesses and ministers, the next. The covenant affirmed the loyalty of the people to the Crown but declared that the king could not re-establish the authority of the episcopate over the church. (The Church of Scotland had a presbyterian form of church government since the Reformation of the sixteenth century under John Knox.)

King Charles foolishly declared everyone who signed the National Covenant a rebel and prepared to move an army into Scotland.

9.1.6 War in Scotland

King Charles called out the militia of the northern counties of England and ordered the English nobility to serve as officers at their own expense. A troop of the King's horses entered Scotland only to find their way blocked by a large Scots army. They returned south of the border without fighting.

Charles signed the Pacification of Berwick with the Scots in June, 1639, by which each side would disband its forces and a new General Assembly of the Church of Scotland and a Scottish Parliament would determine the future constitution of the government. The Church General Assembly confirmed the actions of its predecessor; the Scottish Parliament repealed laws in favor of episcopacy and increased its own powers; and the Scottish army remained in existence.

9.1.7 The Short Parliament

For the first time in eleven years the King convened the English Parliament to vote new taxes for the war with Scotland. Instead the Commons presented to the king a long list of grievances since 1629. These included violations of the rights of Parliament; of civil rights; of changes in church order and government; and of rights of property ownership. In anger the king again dissolved Parliament, which had met only from April 13 to May 5, 1640.

9.1.8 The Scots Invade

The Scots invaded the two northern counties of Northumberland and Durham unopposed. Charles called a Great Council of Lords such as had not met in England for over two hundred years. They arranged a treaty with the Scots to leave things as they were.

9.1.9 *The Long Parliament*

The king was cornered: he had no money, no army, and no popular support. He summoned the Parliament to meet in November 1640. The Commons immediately moved to impeach one of the king's principal ministers, Thomas Wentworth, Earl of Strafford.

Strafford's trial began in March 1641, and lasted three weeks without a verdict. He was accused of treason for subverting the fundamental laws of the realm with an arbitrary and tyrannical government. Treason was traditionally defined as an offense against the king, so the indictment read instead that he was guilty of "treason against the nation."

With mobs in the street and with rumors of an army enroute to London to dissolve Parliament, a bare majority of an under-strength House of Lords passed a bill of attainder to execute the Earl. Agonizingly distraught, but fearing mob violence and Parliament itself, the king signed the bill and Strafford was executed. Archbishop William Laud was also arrested, and eventually tried and executed in 1645.

The House of Commons passed a series of laws to strengthen its position and to better protect civil and religious rights. The Triennial Act provided that no more than three years should pass between Parliaments. An act provided that the current Parliament should not be dissolved without its own consent. Various hated laws, taxes, and institutions were abolished: the Star Chamber, the High Commission, power of the Privy Council to deal with property rights. Ship money, a form of tax, was abolished and tonnage duties were permitted only for a short time. The courts of common law were to remain supreme over the king's courts.

The Commons was ready to remove the power of the king

over the Church of England, but there was disagreement over what form the state church would take: episcopal, presbyterian, or congregational. Puritans were in the majority.

9.1.10 *Rebellion in Ireland and the Grand Remonstrance*

Irish Catholics murdered thousands of their Protestant neighbors. The Commons immediately voted funds for a large army, but questions remained whether it was to be a Parliamentary army or a royal army under the control of the king.

The Grand Remonstrance listed 204 clauses of grievances against the king and demanded that all officers and ministers of the state be approved by Parliament.

9.1.11 *The English Civil War Begins*

With mobs in the streets and gentlemen carrying swords to protect themselves, men began identifying themselves as Cavaliers, in favor of the king, or Roundheads, if they supported Parliament.

In one of his most foolish actions as king, Charles then ordered his Attorney General to prepare impeachment proceedings against five of the leading Puritans in the House of Commons. When the House refused to surrender their members to the custody of the king, Charles went in person to Parliament with four hundred soldiers to arrest the five members. While the five slipped away from Westminster to London, mobs turned out into the streets, including four thousand from Buckinghamshire who sought to defend their hero, Sir John Hotham.

The king withdrew to Hampton Court and sent the Queen to France for safety. In March 1642, Charles II went to York and the English Civil War began.

9.1.12 *The Division of the Country*

To some extent every locality was divided between supporters of the king and supporters of Parliament. Geographically, though, the north and west of England sided with the king, and the south and east, with Parliament. The Midlands was competitive between them.

Eighty great nobles sided with the king, thirty against him. The majority of the gentry supported the king, a large minority were for Parliament. The yeomen tended to side with the gentry of their areas; the peasants wanted to avoid the fighting.

A few London merchants were Royalists, but most businessmen in various towns sided with Parliament. London, which was strongly Presbyterian, supplied parliament with many men and much money.

Parliament had two great advantages:

1) The navy and merchant marine supported Parliament. They brought in munitions and revenue from customs as foreign trade continued. They hindered the coastal towns behind the king's lines.

2) Parliament also had control of the wealthier and more strategic areas, including London, and were able to secure the three principal arsenals: London, Hull, and Portsmouth.

9.1.13 *The King Attacks London*

Charles put together a sizeable force with a strong cavalry and moved on London, winning several skirmishes. He entered Oxford but was beaten back from London. Oxford then became his headquarters for the rest of the war.

9.1.14 *Oliver Cromwell*

Oliver Cromwell, a gentleman farmer from Huntingdon, led the parliamentary troops to victory, first with his cavalry, which eventually numbered eleven hundred, and then as lieutenant general in command of the well-discliplined and well-trained New Model Army.

9.1.15 *Early Stages of the War*

The early part of the war went in favor of the king. Lincolnshire, Cornwall, and Devon were occupied by two of the king's armies in 1643. The Queen returned from France with reinforcements and supplies. The king planned a three-pronged assault on London, but was beaten back by the Earl of Essex. Charles sought allies among Irish Catholics and the parliament sought aid from Presbyterian Scotland.

In January 1644, a well-equipped Scottish army of 21,000 crossed into England, thereby greatly upsetting the military balance. The Duke of Newcastle, the king's general was forced into York and there besieged. Prince Rupert came to his rescue from the west, but precipitated the battle of Marston Moor in July 1644. Cromwell decisively defeated the king's cavalry in a royalist disaster. The north was now in Parliamentary hands.

The king was not beaten yet, however. James Graham, the Marquis of Montrose, raised troops for the king in the Scottish Highlands, much to the consternation of the Lowlands Scots.

Parliament reconstructed and improved its army, giving Oliver Cromwell the top command. In June 1645, Charles marched into enemy territory and was crushed by Cromwell's "Ironsides" at Naseby. The king was then a fugitive and surrendered himself to the Scots in May 1646.

9.1.16 *Controversy Between Parliament and the Army*

The majority of Parliament were Presbyterians, wanting to extend the Scottish National Covenant idea to England. Many soldiers, however, were Independents who believed in democracy politically and congregational control of the church.

During the Civil War, under the authority of Parliament the Westminster Assembly convened to write a statement of faith for the Church of England that was Reformed or Presbyterian in content. Ministers and laymen from both England and Scotland participated for six years and wrote the Westminster Confession of Faith, still a vital part of Presbyterian theology.

When the war ended, Parliament ordered the army to disband without receiving the pay due them. The army refused to disband and in 1647 Parliament sought to disperse them by force. The plan was to bring the Scottish army into England and use it against the men who had won the war.

The army refused to obey Parliament and arrested the king when he was brought across the border. In August the army occupied London and some of their leaders wrote an "Agreement of the People" to be presented to the House of Commons. It called for a democratic republic with a written constitution with elections every two years, equal electoral districts with universal manhood suffrage, freedom of conscience, freedom from impressment, equality before the law, and no office of king or House of Lords.

9.1.17 *The Death of the King*

On the night of November 11, 1647, the king escaped from Hampton Court and went to the Isle of Wight. He had made a secret agreement with the Scots that he would establish Presbyterianism throughout England and Scotland if they would restore him to his throne.

The Second Civil War followed in 1648 but it consisted only of scattered local uprisings and the desertion of part of the English fleet.

The Scots invaded England but were defeated by Cromwell at Preston, Wigan, and Warrington in the northwest of England. After these victories the English army took control. London was again occupied. The army arrested 45 Presbyterian members of Parliament and excluded the rest and admitted only about 60 Independents, acting as the "Rump Parliament."

The Army then tried Charles Stuart, formerly king of England, and sentenced him to death for treason. They charged him with illegal deaths and with governing in a tyrannical way instead of by the constitutional system of limited power that he had inherited. The execution of the king particularly shocked the Scots because the English had specifically promised not to take the king's life when the Scots delivered him into English hands.

9.2 THE COMMONWEALTH AND THE PROTECTORATE (1649 – 59)

9.2.1 *The Commonwealth* (1649 – 53)

After the execution of the king, the Parliament abolished the office of king and House of Lords. The new form of government was to be a Commonwealth, or Free State, governed by the representatives of the people in Parliament.

The people, however, were not represented in Parliament. Many large areas of the country had no representatives in Parliament. The ninety Independents that controlled Parliament did not want elections.

The Commonwealth was in effect a continuation of the Long Parliament under a different name. Parliament was more powerful than ever because there was neither king nor House of Lords to act as a check.

The Commons appointed a Council of State and entrusted it with administrative power. Thirty-one of its forty-one members were also members of Parliament.

9.2.2 Opposition to the Commonwealth

Royalists and Presbyterians were both against Parliament for the lack of broad representation and for regicide. The Army was greatly dissatisfied that elections were not held, when popular representation was one of the promises of the Civil War.

The death of the king provoked a violent reaction abroad. In Russia the Czar imprisoned English merchants. In Holland Royalist privateers were allowed to refit. An English ambassador at the Hague and another in Madrid were murdered by Royalists. France was openly hostile.

Surrounded by enemies, the Commonwealth became a military state with a standing army of 44,000. The army, with career soldiers, was probably the best in Europe, and the best paid. Forty warships were built in three years. The North American and West Indian colonies were forced to accept the government of the Commonwealth.

9.2.3 Ireland

In the summer of 1649 Cromwell landed in Dublin with a well-equipped army of 12,000. Despite a coalition of Protestant Royalists and Irish Catholics, the Irish did not put together an army to oppose him. Instead they relied on fortresses for safety.

Drogheda was the scene of the first massacre when Cromwell ordered the slaughter of the entire garrison of 2800. Another massacre took place at Wexford.

This campaign of terror induced many towns to surrender; by the end of 1649 the southern and eastern coast was in English hands. In 1650, Cromwell captured Kilkenny and left the rest of the conquest to others.

The lands of all Roman Catholics who had taken part in the war were confiscated and given in payment to Protestant soldiers and others. Two-thirds of the land in Ireland changed hands, controlled mostly by Protestant landlords.

9.2.4 Scotland

Scottish Presbyterians, offended by the Independents' control of the English Parliament and by the execution of the king, proclaimed Charles II as their king. Charles accepted the National Covenant and agreed to govern a Presbyterian realm.

On September 3, 1650, Cromwell defeated the Scots at Dunbar, Near Edinburgh and killed 3,000, taking 10,000 prisoner. The next year King Charles II led a Scots army into England, which was annihilated almost to the last man at Worcester. Charles was a fugitive for six weeks before escaping to France.

9.2.5 The Protectorate (1653 – 59)

When it became clear that Parliament intended to stay in office permanently without new elections, Cromwell took troops to Parliament and forced all members to leave, thus dissolving the Parliament.

Cromwell had no desire to rule either as king or military

dictator and called for new elections – but not from the old system. Most were chosen by Independent or Puritan churches.

Cromwell then agreed to serve as Lord Protector with a Council of State, and a Parliament. The new government permitted religious liberty, except for Catholics and Anglicans.

England was not strongly opposed to military rule, particularly after Cromwell divided the country into twelve districts with a major general in charge of each.

Oliver Cromwell died on September 3, 1658. After Cromwell's death a new Parliament was elected under the old historic franchise.

9.3   THE RESTORATION (1660 – 1688)

The new Parliament restored the monarchy, but the Puritan Revolution clearly showed that the English constitutional system required a limited monarchy, with the king as chief executive – but not as absolute ruler. Parliament in 1660 was in a far stronger position in relationship to the king than it ever had been before.

9.3.1 *Charles II (1660 – 85)*

Thirty years of age at the Restoration, the new king was dissolute, lazy, affable, intelligent, a liar, and a cunning deceiver. He loved the sea and the navy and was interested in science and trade. Because he had so little interest in religion, he was willing to be tolerant.

While still on the Continent, Charles II issued the Declaration of Breda in which he agreed to abide by Parliament's decisions on the postwar settlement.

9.3.2 *The Convention Parliament* (1660)

Parliament pardoned all those who fought in the Civil War except for fifty people listed by name. Of these, twelve were executed for "regicide."

Royalists whose lands had been confiscated by the Puritans were allowed to recover their lands through the courts, but those who had sold them should receive no compensation. That meant that both Roundheads and Cavaliers would be the landowners of England.

To raise money for the government, Parliament granted the king income from customs duties and an excise on beer, ale, tea, and coffee. Feudalism was largely abolished.

9.3.3 *The Clarendon Code*

Of England's 9,000 parish churches, 2,000 were pastored by Presbyterian ministers and 400 by Independents, and the rest by Anglicans. The Cavalier Parliament, elected early in 1661, sought to drive out all Puritans and exclude them from public and ecclesiastical life.

The Corporation Act of 1661 excluded from local government any one who refused to swear to the unlawfullness of resistance to the king and those who did not receive communion according to the pattern of the Church of England. The Act of Uniformity in 1662 issued a new Prayer Book and ordered ministers either to accept it or resign their positions and livelihood. 1,200 pastors refused and vacated their churches.

The Conventicle Act of 1664 and 1670 imposed harsh penalties on those who attended religious services which did not follow the forms of the Anglican Church. The Five-Mile Act, 1665, prohibited ministers from coming within five miles of a parish from which they had been removed as pastor. A licensing act permitted the Archbishop of Canterbury and the bishop of London to control the press and the publishing of books.

The effect of all this was to divide England into two great groups – the Anglican Church and nonconformists:

1) The church was purged of Puritans and regained its property. It levied tithes and controlled education at all levels.

2) Nonconformists were excluded from the universities, from government, from many professions, and from membership in the House of Commons. Some, of course, became Anglicans outwardly but did not believe what they professed. Nonconformists became shopkeepers, artisans, small farmers, merchants, bankers, and manufacturers. Their diligence, thrift, and self-discipline brought prosperity. They were strengthened by the rise of Methodism in the eighteenth century.

9.3.4 Disasters for England

War with the Dutch cost enormously in ships and money. The bubonic plague hit London in 1665, killing 68,000. The Great Fire of London in 1666 destroyed 13,000 homes, 84 churches, and many public buildings, none covered by insurance.

9.3.5 Scotland's Independence

Scotland regained here independence at the restoration of Charles II in 1660. The Earl of Middleton was made the King's Commissioner in the Scottish Parliament and commander of the army in Scotland. Some of the Scottish Presbyterian ministers reminded the king of the National Covenant of 1638 and of his own covenant-oath in 1651 pledging that Scotland be governed according to Presbyterian polity and principles.

The king arrested the Marquis of Argyle, a Presbyterian and leader of the Covanenters. He was charged with treason for his "compliance with Cromwell's government." Argyle and James Guthrie were both executed.

Charles II declared himself head of the Church of Scotland and decreed that the episcopal form of hierarchical church government would be used in Scotland.

In 1661 the Scottish Parliament declared that the National Covenant was no longer binding and prohibited anyone to renew any covenant or oath without royal permission.

Samuel Rutherford, influential author of *Lex Rex* and Principal of St. Mary's College, St. Andrews, was cited by the Privy Council for treason in 1661, but died before trial could be held.

A dictatorship was established in Scotland to enforce episcopacy and rule by approved bishops. The government demanded absolute obedience and used illegal detention. Drastic fines were levied on hundreds of people suspected of being sympathetic to the Covenanters. Presbyterianism was outlawed and hundreds of ministers lost their positions.

By 1666 the covenanters finally took to arms against oppression and captured the commanding general at Dumfries.

Perhaps as many as 18,000 ordinary people died for the cause of religious liberty in the persecution that followed. Dragoons were sent to prevent people from meeting in the files and in "unlicensed" homes for the purpose of worshipping God and studying the Bible. Others were fined for not attending the parish church.

Archbishop James Sharp was assassinated by a group of over-zealous Covenanters on May 3, 1679. Covenanting leaders immediately repudiated the action, but it led to pitched battles between the king's troops and covenanters.

The last two years of Charles II reign in Scotland were known as the Killing Times because of the wholesale slaughter of hundreds who were shot down without trial if they refused to take the oath of objuration of the Covenant.

Charles II died on February 5, 1685, in his 56th year and received Roman Catholic absolution on his deathbed.

9.3.6   *James II (1685 – 88)*

The new king, fifty-one years of age, was the brother of Charles II. He had served as Lord Admiral and commanded an English fleet against the Dutch.

James II began his reign in a strong position. The Whigs were weak and the Tories were in overwhelming strength in Parliament. They immediately voted the king income from customs for life.

James II was a strong Roman Catholic and was determined to return England to Catholicism. He proceeded to appoint Catholics to many of the high positions in his government. In 1685, James created a court of Ecclesiastical Commission with power over the clergy and suspended the bishop of London from office. Three colleges at the University of Oxford were put under Roman Catholic Rule. (Oxford was an Anglican and Tory stronghold so the king was jeopardizing his own supporters.)

In April 1687 King James issued a Declaration of Indulgence which declared both Catholics and nonconformists free to worship in public and to hold office. This was a bold move but the nonconformists knew that the intent was to enable Catholics to eventually control the government. So instead of supporting the king, they secured a promise from Anglicans that they would eventually be given toleration.

9.4   THE GLORIOUS REVOLUTION OF 1688

The leaders of Parliament were not at all willing to sacrifice the constitutional gains of the English Civil War and return to an absolute monarchy. Two events in 1688 goaded them to action:

1) In May James reissued the Declaration of Indulgence with the command that it be read on two successive Sundays in every parish church. Archbishop Bancroft and six bishops petitioned the king to withdraw his command and printed and distributed their petition. This was a technical violation of the law and the king ordered them prosecuted for publishing a seditious libel against his government. When a London jury reached a verdict of "not guilty," it was clear that the king did not have popular support.

2) On June 10, 1688, a son was born to the king and his queen, Mary of Modena. They had been married for fifteen years and their other children had died. As long as James was childless by his second wife, the throne would go to one of his Protestant daughters, Mary or Anne. The birth of a son, who would be raised Roman Catholic, changed the picture completely.

A group of Whig and Tory leaders, speaking for both houses of Parliament, invited William and Mary to assume the throne of England. William III was Stadtholder of Holland and son of Mary, the daughter of Charles I. Mary II was the daughter of James II by his first wife, Anne Hyde. So they were both in the Stuart dynasty.

William was willing to assume the English throne only if he had popular support and only if accompanied by his own Dutch troops, despite the irritation their presence would cause in England.

The Dutch feared that King Louis XIV would attack Holland while their army was in England, but the French attacked the Palatinate instead and eliminated that fear. Louis XIV offered James II the French fleet but James declined what would have been very little help. King Louis thought that William's invasion would result in a civil war which would neutralize both England and Holland, but he was mistaken. On November 5, 1688, William and his army landed at Torbay in Devon. King James offered many concessions, but it was too late. He advanced with his army to Salisbury, then returned to London, then fled to France.

William assumed temporary control of the government and summoned a free Parliament, which met in February 1689. Whigs and Tories met in a conciliatory spirit though party differences soon were evident:

1) The Whigs wanted a declaration that the throne was vacant in order to break the royal succession and give the king a parliamentary title.

2) The Tories declared that the king had abdicated so as not to admit that they had deposed him.

3) William and Mary were declared joint sovereigns, with the administration given to William.

The English Bill of Rights (1689) declared the following:

1) The king could not be a Roman Catholic.

2) A standing army in time of peace was illegal without Parliamentary approval.

3) Taxation was illegal without Parliamentary consent.

4) Excessive bail and cruel and unusual punishments were prohibited.

5) Right to trial by jury was guaranteed.

6) Free elections to Parliament would be held.

The Toleration Act (1689) granted the right of public worship to Protestant nonconformists but did not permit them to hold office. The Act did not extend liberty to Catholics or Unitarians, but normally they were left alone.

The Trials for Treason Act (1696) stated that a person accused of treason should be shown the accusations against him, should have the advice of counsel, and should not be convicted except upon the testimony of two independent witnesses.

Freedom of the press was permitted, but with very strict libel laws.

Control of finances was to be in the hands of Commons, including military appropriations. There would no longer be uncontrolled grants to the King.

The Act of Settlement in 1701 provided that if William or Anne should die without children (Queen Mary had died in 1694) the throne should descend, not to the exiled Stuarts, but to Sophia, Electress Dowager of Hanover, a granddaughter of King James I, or to her Protestant heirs.

Judges were made independent of the Crown. Thus, England declared itself a limited monarchy and a Protestant nation.

9.5 QUEEN ANNE (1702 – 14)

Much of Queen Anne's reign was occupied with the War of the Spanish Succession (1702 – 13). The reign of Queen Anne is also called the Augustan Age of English elegance and wealth. Anne was a devout Anglican, a semi-invalid who ate too much and was too slow-witted to be an effective ruler. She had sixteen children, none of whom survived her.

The most important achievement of Queen Anne's reign was the Act of Union (1707), which united Scotland and England into one kingdom. The Scots gave up their Parliament and sent forty-five members to the English House of Commons and sixteen to the House of Lords. Presbyterianism was retained as the national church.

9.6 EIGHTEENTH CENTURY ENGLAND

Following the Act of Settlement in 1701 and Queen Anne's death in 1714, the House of Hanover inherited the English throne in order to insure that a Protestant would rule the realm.

The Hanover dynasty was as follows:

1) George I (1714 – 1727).

2) George II (1727 – 60).

3) George III (1760 – 1820).

4) George IV (1820 – 30).

5) William IV (1830 – 37).

6) Queen Victoria (1837 – 1901).

Because of the English Civil War, the Commonwealth, and the Glorious Revolution of 1688, the Hanovers were willing to rule as King-in-Parliament, which meant that to rule England, the king and his ministers had to have the support of a majority in Parliament. Sir Robert Walpole, who served forty-two years in the English government, created the office of Prime Minister, a vital link between King and Parliament. Other famous eighteenth century prime ministers were the Duke of Newcastle, George Grenville, William Pitt, Earl of Chatham, Lord North, and William Pitt the Younger.

International events in which Britain was involved in the eighteenth century are discussed in Chapter 1.

Other topics of importance were as follows:

1) The loss of England's North American colonies in the American War for Independence (1775 – 83) was a major blow to the British Empire.

2) Ireland received very harsh treatment under British rule during this period.

In March 1689, James II arrived in Dublin with 7,000 French troops and was joined by Irish Catholics seeking independence from England. Protestants fled to Londonderry which withstood a siege of 105 days. In June 1690, William landed in Ireland with an army of 36,000 and at the Battle of Boyne completely defeated James, who fled to France.

Repercussions in Ireland were harsh: no Catholic could hold office, sit in the Irish Parliament, or vote for its members. He could enter no learned profession except medicine. He was subject to discriminatory taxation. He could not purchase land or hold long leases.

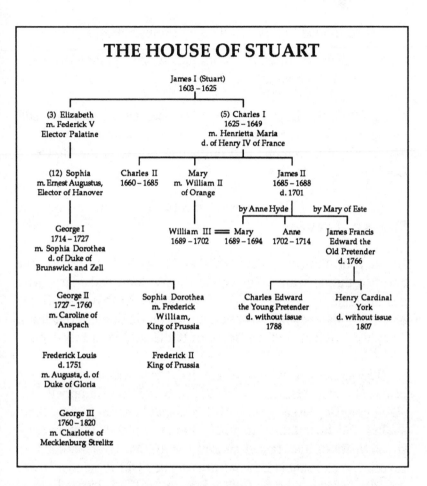

THE HOUSE OF STUART

James I (Stuart)
1603 – 1625

(3) Elizabeth
m. Federick V
Elector Palatine

(5) Charles I
1625 – 1649
m. Henrietta Maria
d. of Henry IV of France

(12) Sophia
m. Ernest Augustus,
Elector of Hanover

Charles II
1660 – 1685

Mary
m. William II
of Orange

James II
1685 – 1688
d. 1701

by Anne Hyde   by Mary of Este

George I
1714 – 1727
m. Sophia Dorothea
d. of Duke of
Brunswick and Zell

William III === Mary
1689 – 1702   1689 – 1694

Anne
1702 – 1714

James Francis
Edward the
Old Pretender
d. 1766

George II
1727 – 1760
m. Caroline of
Anspach

Sophia Dorothea
m. Frederick
William,
King of Prussia

Charles Edward
the Young Pretender
d. without issue
1788

Henry Cardinal
York
d. without issue
1807

Frederick Louis
d. 1751
m. Augusta, d. of
Duke of Gloria

Frederick II
King of Prussia

George III
1760 – 1820
m. Charlotte of
Mecklenburg Strelitz

The American War for Independence gave hope to the Irish that they might obtain autonomy or independence. British troops were withdrawn from Ireland to be sent to America and an Irish militia was formed.

The British did grant concessions to the Irish between 1778 and 1783:

1) Roman Catholics could inherit property and hold long-term leases.

2) The Irish Parliament was given its independence but

continued to be controlled by Protestants.

3) Executive officials continued to be appointed by the English Crown.

In 1800, the Irish Parliament was persuaded to vote itself out of existence in exchange for one hundred seats in the British House of Commons and thirty-two places in the House of Lords.

Scotland was the scene of Jacobin efforts to restore the Stuarts to the throne.

In 1688 the Scots declared that James had "forfeited" the Scottish throne which they offered to William and Mary, with the understanding that Scotland would be Presbyterian. Some of the Highland clans, however, turned out in defense of James. They were defeated at the Battle of Killiecrankie in July 1689.

The settlement with William and Mary was marred by the brutal Glencoe Massacre of 1692, in which the Campbell clan slaughtered a large group of Macdonalds after giving them shelter and hospitality. In 1715, James II's son, then twenty-seven years of age, raised an army of 10,000 Highlanders in a revolt. James Francis Edward Stuart (the "Old Pretender") was soundly defeated and he fled to France. In 1745, James Francis Stuart's son, Charles Edward, the "Young Pretender", then in his middle twenties, obtained two ships from the French and sought to incite an uprising in Scotland, winning lasting fame as "Bonnie Prince Charlie."

His spirit and ambition won him the backing of several Highland chiefs. He was a natural leader and his men respected him for enduring the hardships of the common soldier.

Charles was able to capture the city of Edinburgh, but not

the fortified castle. Soon he was forced to retreat north to Inverness. At Culloden, in April 1746, he was completely defeated. The rebellion was followed with harsh English reprisals. There were many executions and parts of the Highlands were devastated. The Highlanders were disarmed and even the Highland kilt and tartan were forbidden.

CHAPTER 10

SCANDINAVIA

10.1 SWEDEN IN THE THIRTY YEARS' WAR

King Gustavus Adolphus drove the Imperial forces from Pomerania in 1630. Swedish troops occupied all of Bohemia, organized a new Protestant Union, and invaded Bavaria. Gustavus Adolphus was killed in 1632 in the Battle of Lutzen.

In the fall of 1634, Imperial forces decisively defeated the Swedish army at Nordlingen. The Treaty of Prague (1635) restored Catholic and Protestant lands to their status as of 1627.

Catholic France allied with Protestant Sweden against the Hapsburg Empire during the last phase of the war from 1635 – 1648. Sweden acquired western Pomerania as part of the Peace of Westphalia (1648), ending the Thirty Years' War.

10.2 SWEDISH EMPIRE

The high point of Swedish power in the Baltics was in the 1650's. Population of the Swedish Empire including the German provinces was only three million, half of whom were Swedish.

Sweden was not a large or productive country. Maintaining a strong standing army proved to be too much of a strain on the economy. Sweden sought to control the trade of the Baltic Sea with its important naval stores, but even at the height of Swedish power only 10% of the ships in the Baltic trade were Swedish; 65% were Dutch.

Swedish provinces in the Baltic and in Germany were impossible to defend against a strong continental power such as Russia, Prussia, or Austria.

10.3 POLITICAL SITUATION

After the death of Gustavus Adolphus in 1632, the government was effectively controlled by an oligarchy of the nobility ruling in the name of the Vasa dynasty.

Christina, the daughter of Gustavus Adolphus, became queen at six years of age and ruled from 1632 to 54. At age twenty-eight, she abdicated the throne to her cousin and devoted the rest of her life to the Catholic religion and art.

Charles X Gustavus reigned from 1654 to 60 during the First Northern War against Poland, Russia, and Denmark.

Poland ceded Livonia to Sweden by the *Treaty of Olivia* (1660). Denmark surrendered to Sweden the southern part of the Scandinavian Peninsula by the *Treaty of Copenhagen* (1660).

Charles XI (1660 – 97) became king at age eleven. When he came of age, he spent the rest of his life attempting to regain

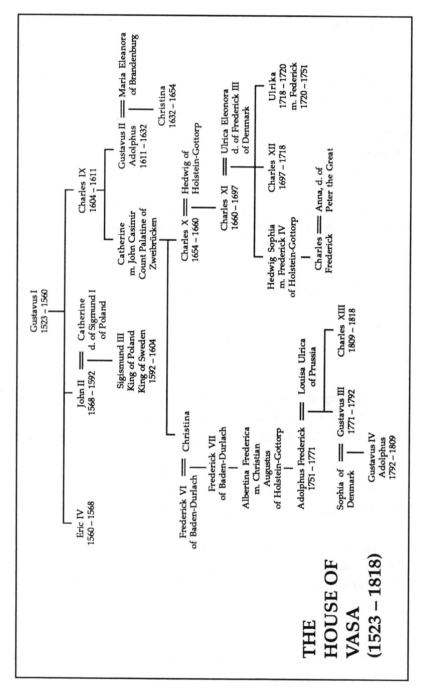

THE
HOUSE OF
VASA
(1523 – 1818)

Gustavus I
1523 – 1560

Eric IV
1560 – 1568

John II
1568 – 1592
═ Catherine
d. of Sigmund I
of Poland

Charles IX
1604 – 1611

Sigismund III
King of Poland
King of Sweden
1592 – 1604

Catherine
m. John Casimir
Count Palatine of
Zweibrücken

Gustavus II
Adolphus
1611 – 1632
═ Maria Eleanora
of Brandenburg

Christina
1632 – 1654

Charles X ═ Hedwig of
1654 – 1660   Holstein-Gottorp

Charles XI
1660 – 1697
═ Ulrica Eleonora
d. of Frederick III
of Denmark

Hedwig Sophia
m. Frederick IV
of Holstein-Gottorp

Charles ═ Anna, d. of
Frederick   Peter the Great

Charles XII
1697 – 1718

Ulrika
1718 – 1720
m. Federick
1720 – 1751

Frederick VI ═ Christina
of Baden-Durlach

Frederick VII
of Baden-Durlach

Albertina Frederica
m. Christian
Augustus
of Holstein-Gottorp

Adolphus Frederick
1751 – 1771
═ Louisa Ulrica
of Prussia

Sophia of ═ Gustavus III
Denmark   1771 – 1792

Charles XIII
1809 – 1818

Gustavus IV
Adolphus
1792 – 1809

powers lost to the Council. For this he secured the aid of the Lower Estates of the Riksdag who in 1693 declared that Charles XI was "absolute sovereign King, responsible to no one on earth, but with power and might as his command to rule and govern the realm as a Christian monarch." This was in dramatic contrast to the centuries' long struggles in Holland and England to constitutionally limit their kings.

King Charles XII (1697 – 1718) came to the throne at age 15 and reigned for twenty-one years. He spent most of his life at war and was an outstanding military leader in the Great Northern War (1700 – 1721).

Denmark, Saxony, Poland, and Russia formed an alliance to destroy the Swedish Empire. In February, 1700, Poland attacked Swedish Livonia and Denmark invaded Holstein. The Swedish navy defeated the Danes and attacked Copenhagen, forcing Denmark to make peace.

Charles then shifted his attention to Estonia and routed a Russian invasion in the Battle of Narva, inflicting heavy losses. Charles was then eighteen years of age.

The next several years were spent fighting in Poland, defeating both Poles and Russians, but in 1709 the Russians, outnumbering the Swedish forces two-to-one, defeated them. Peter the Great then took the Baltic provinces of Livonia and Estonia from Sweden.

Years of warfare, poor government, and high taxes finally led to Charles XII's alienation from his people. In 1718 he was killed by a stray bullet.

10.4 EIGHTEENTH CENTURY SWEDEN

The loss of the Empire meant a move to a more democratic, limited monarchy and the new freedom led to a sharp increase in peasant enterprises and independence. The Swedish economy prospered.

By 1756 parliament considered itself the sovereign Estates of the realm and many civil liberties were established. Principal decisions of government were made by the Riskdag (Parliament).

Under Gustavus III there was a temporary return to royal absolutism until he was assassinated in 1792.

10.5 SCANDINAVIAN RELATIONSHIPS

Finland was part of the Swedish Empire in the seventeenth century and Norway was part of Denmark. In the early nineteenth century Sweden gave up Finland but acquired Norway as an autonomous part of a union of the two nations.

10.6 DENMARK

Frederick III (1648 – 70), established himself as absolute ruler.

Frederick IV (1699 – 1730) fought in the Northern War and achieved a rough parity in the Baltic with Sweden, but accepted Swedish control of the south of the Scandinavian Peninsula.

Christian VII experimented with both enlightened despotism and reforms allowing more civil liberties and economic freedoms to the Danish people.

CHAPTER 11

RUSSIA OF THE ROMANOVS

11.1 BACKGROUND TO 17TH CENTURY

11.1.1 *Ivan III* (1440 – 1505)

Ivan III, "Ivan the Great," put an end in 1480 to Mongol domination over Russia. He married Sophie Paleologus (1472), the niece of the last emperor of Constantinople. (The Byzantine Empire was conquered by the Ottoman Turks in 1453). Ivan took the title of Caesar (i.e., *Czar*) as heir of the Eastern Roman Empire (i.e., Byzantine Empire). He encouraged the Eastern Orthodox Church and called Moscow the "Third Rome", and many Greek scholars, craftsmen, architects, and artists were brought to Russia.

11.1.2 *Ivan IV* (1533 – 84)

Ivan IV, "Ivan the Terrible," grandson of Ivan III, began westernizing Russia.

A contemporary of Queen Elizabeth, he welcomed both the

English and the Dutch and opened new trade routes to Moscow and the Caspian Sea. English merchant adventurers opened Archangel on the White Sea and provided a link with the outer world free from Polish domination.

The "Time of Troubles" followed the death of Ivan IV in 1584 when the ruling Muscovite family died out. The Time of Troubles was a period of turmoil, famine, power struggles, and invasions from Poland.

11.2 THE ROMANOV DYNASTY

The Romanov dynasty ruled Russia from 1613 to 1917. Stability returned to Russia in 1613 when the *Semski Sobor* (estates general representing the Russian Orthodox Church, landed gentry, townspeople, and a few peasants) elected Michael Romanov as Czar from 1613 to 1645.

Russia, with a standing army of 70,000, was involved in a series of unsuccessful wars with Poland, Sweden, and Turkey. In 1654, Russia annexed the Ukraine with its rich farmlands. The Ukranians were to be granted full autonomy, but were not.

It was under Michael Romanov that Russia continued its expansion into contiguous territory and created an enormous empire across Asia to the Pacific. Westernization, begun under Ivan IV, continued under Michael Romanov.

The Russian army was trained by westerners, mostly Scotsmen. Weapons were purchased from Sweden and Holland. Four Lutheran and Reformed Churches and a German school were established in Moscow. Western skills and technology, western clothes and customs were accepted in Russia. By the end of the 17th century, 20,000 Europeans lived in Russia, developing trade and manufacturing, practicing medicine,

THE HOUSE OF ROMANOV (1613 – 1801)

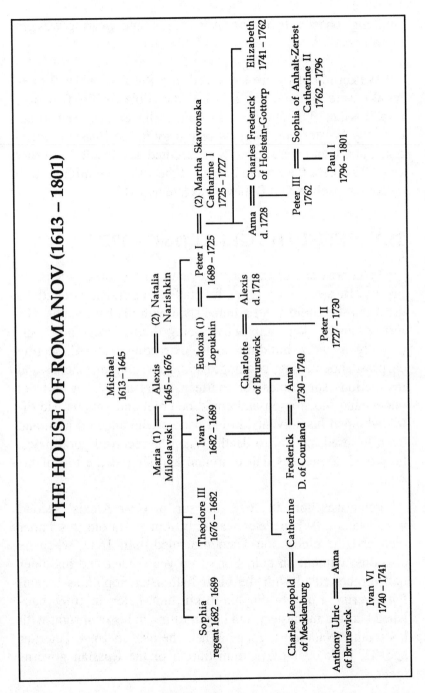

smoking tobacco, trimming their beards, and wearing western clothing.

Western books were translated into Russian. In 1649 three monks were appointed to translate the Bible for the first time into Russian. The *Raskolniki* (Old Believers) refused to accept any Western innovations or liturgy in the Russian Orthodox Church and were severely persecuted as a result. In twenty years 20,000 of them were burned at the stake, but millions still called themselves Old Believers as late as 1917.

11.3   PETER THE GREAT (1682 – 1725)

Peter was one of the most extraordinary people in Russian history. He was nearly seven feet tall with physical strength so great that he could bend a horse shoe with his bare hands. His restless energy kept him active doing things incessantly, perpetually at work building boats, extracting teeth, dissecting corpses, shoemaking, cooking, etching, writing dispatches and instructions sometimes for fourteen hours a day. He did not understand moderation and could be cruel and vicious. He often whipped his servants, killed people who angered him, and even tortured his son to death. When he received good news, he would sometimes dance around and sing at the top of his voice.

Peter was born in 1672, the son of Czar Alexis' second wife, Natalia. When Peter was only four years old, his father died and the oldest son Theodore ruled until 1682, when he also died without an heir. For seven years Peter and his older half-brother ruled with the older half-sister Sophia as regent. Discovering a plot by Sophia to kill him, Peter, in 1689, banished her to a monastery and began ruling in his own right with his mother Natalia as regent. When she died in 1694, Peter, at age 22, took over the administration of the Russian government.

The driving ambition of Peter the Great's life was to modernize Russia and he needed the West to accomplish that. At the same time he wanted to compete with the great powers of Europe on equal terms.

Peter visited western Europe (in disguise!) in order to study the techniques and culture of the West. He worked as a carpenter in shipyards; attended gunnery school; and visited hospitals and factories. He sent back to Russia large numbers of European technicians and craftsmen to train Russians and to build factories, some of which were larger than any in the West. By the end of Peter's reign Russia produced more iron than England (though not more than Sweden or Germany).

11.3.1 *Wars of Peter the Great*

Peter built up the army through conscription and a 25-year term of enlistment. He gave flintlocks and bayonets to his troops instead of the old muskets and pikes. Artillery was improved and discipline enforced. By the end of his reign Russia had a standing army of 210,000 out of a population of only 13 million. Peter also developed the Russian Navy.

In 1696, Peter sailed the fleet of boats down the Don River and took Azov on the Black Sea from the Turks.

11.3.2 *The Great Northern War* (1700 – 1721)

In 1699 Peter allied with Poland and Denmark against Sweden.

Charles XII, the 18-year-old Swedish king, defeated the Russian army of 35,000, capturing its artillery and most of its senior officers.

The main Swedish effort, though, was against Poland, but

the Swedish war lasted for twenty years. In 1706 Sweden again defeated Russia at Grodno, but in 1709 Peter won at Poltava.

Treaty of Nystad (1721) ended the war. Russia returned Finland. Livonia (Latvia) and Estonia became part of the Russian Empire. Russia now had possessions on the Baltic Sea and a "window on the West."

11.3.3 *St. Petersburg*

The building of this great city (formerly Leningrad) out of a wilderness and making it the capital and one of the two principal cities of Russia was one of Peter's crowning achievements. Construction began in 1703, supervised by the Czar himself and done by conscripted labor.

Peter sought to make St. Petersburg look like Amsterdam. It became cosmopolitan, lively city with French theater and Italian opera. His palace imitated Versailles with its terraces, fountains, cascade, art gallery, and park. St. Petersburg was built mostly of stone and brick rather than from traditional Russian wood.

The Czar ordered a specific number of noble families to move to St. Petersburg and build their houses according to Peter's plans. At Peter's death in 1725, St. Petersburg had a population of 75,000, the largest city in northern Europe.

11.3.4 *Reforms Under Peter the Great*

The Czar ruled by decree (*ukase*). Government officials and nobles acted under government authority, but there was no representative body.

All land-owners owed lifetime service to the state, either in the army, the civil service, or at court. In return for government service they received land and serfs to work their fields.

Conscription required each village to send recruits for the Russian army. By 1709 Russia manufactured most of its own weapons and had an effective artillery.   '

The Russian navy, mostly on the Baltic, grew to a fleet of 850 ships, but declined sharply after Peter's death.

Taxes were heavy on trade, on sales, on rents, and the government levied a head tax on every male.

State-regulated monopolies brought income to the government, but stultified trade and economic growth so in the long-run were counter-productive economically. Half of the two hundred enterprises begun during Peter's reign were state-owned; the rest were heavily taxed.

Peter sought unsuccessfully to link the main rivers by canals. Thousands died in the effort but only one of his six great canals was completed: St. Petersburg was linked to the Volga by canal in 1732.

The budget of the Russian government at the end of Peter's reign was three times its size at the beginning, 75% of which was spent on the military. Peter established naval, military, and artillery academies.

The Russian Secret Police ferreted out opposition and punished it as subversion.

The Swedish model was followed in organizing the central government. Russia was divided into twelve provinces with a governor in charge to decentralize many of the functions previously done by the national government.

Industrial serfdom mean that workers were brought and sold with the factories and invariably created inferior products.

Russia had a "conditional land tenure" system with the Czar as the theoretical owner of all land in a Russian-style feudal system where both nobility and serfs served the state.

When the Patriarch of the Russian Orthodox Church died in 1700, Peter abolished his authority and began treating the Church as a government department. He eventually gave governing authority to a Holy Synod.

11.4 18th CENTURY RUSSIAN CZARS AFTER PETER THE GREAT

Catherine I, who ruled from 1725 to 27, was the second wife of Peter the Great.

Peter II (1727 – 30) the son of Alexis and grandson of Peter the Great, died at age 15.

Anna (1730 – 40) was dominated by German advisers. Under her rule the war of the Polish Succession (1733 – 35) gave Russia firmer control over Polish affairs. War against the Turks (1736 – 39) gave Azov to Russia once again. Russia agreed not to build a fleet on the Black Sea.

Ivan VI (1740 – 41) was overthrown by a military coup.

Elizabeth (1741 – 62) was the youngest daughter of Peter the Great. This was the Golden Age of the aristocracy as they freed themselves from some of the obligations imposed on them by earlier Czars. Russia entered the Seven Years' War (1756 – 63) during Elizabeth's reign.

THE GROWTH OF RUSSIA, 1725 – 1801

Peter III (1762) was deposed and killed in a military revolt.

Catherine II ("the Great"; 1762 – 96) continued the westernization process begun by Peter the Great. The three partitions of Poland, in 1772, 1793, and 1795 respectively, occurred under Catherine II's rule. Russia also annexed the Crimea and warred with Turkey.

CHAPTER 12

ITALY AND THE PAPACY

12.1 THE PAPACY

For the first time in its long history the Papacy was of secondary importance in European diplomacy. There were a number of factors in the decline of the Papacy:

1) The Protestant Reformation of the sixteenth century and the emergence of many Protestant kingdoms throughout Europe.

2) The emphasis towards limited constitutional government taught in the Protestant Reformation and accepted by many non-Protestants as well.

3) The relatively few sanctions available to the Pope in an international atmosphere of *realpolitik*.

4) The beginnings of secularization of Europe through the growing influence of the Enlightenment.

5) The anti-clericalism associated with the Enlightenment with its desire to reduce the power and economic holdings of the church in traditionally Catholic countries.

Anti-clericalism reached a climax in the French Revolution.

6) The lack of Papal leadership in countering the above. Most of the 17th and 18th century popes were more concerned about administering their own territories than in the wider political milieu.

Pope Innocent X (1644 – 55) protested against the Peace of Westphalia (1648) because it acknowledged the rights of Lutherans and Calvinists in Germany, but the diplomats at Westphalia paid him little attention.

Quiet obscurity characterized the next three popes, Alexander VIII (1655 – 67), Clement IX (1667 – 69), and Clement X (1670 – 76), though they did clash with King Louis XIV over the prerogatives of the Church versus the prerogatives of the Crown, particularly in the appointment of bishops.

Innocent XI (1676 – 89) was scrupulous in financial matters and worked actively against the Turkish invasion of Europe. He subsidized Poland's relief of Vienna in the great campaign against the Turks in 1683.

Clement XI (1700 – 21) sided with France in the War of the Spanish Succession and in the course of the war, the Papal states were invaded by Austria. Clement renewed the condemnation of Jansenism, which had made extraordinary progress in France. (Jansenism was an Augustinian Catholic reform movement akin to Protestant Calvinism in its theology.)

Benedict XIV (1740 – 58), much influenced by the Enlightenment, sought to salvage some of the Church's lost influence in absolute European states by compromising the state's influence in nationally-established Catholic churches.

Clement XIV (1769 – 74) ordered the Jesuit Society dissolved (July 21, 1773).

Pius VI (1775 – 99) felt the full force of French radical anti-clericalism, which finally led to the French invasion of the Papal states in 1796.

12.2   17TH AND 18TH CENTURY ITALY

Italy in the 17th and 18th centuries remained merely a geographic expression divided into small kingdoms, most of which were under foreign domination. Unification of Italy into a national-state did not occur until the mid-nineteenth century.

In the 17th century Spain controlled most of the Italian peninsula. Spain owned Lombardy in the north and Naples, Sicily, and Sardinia. Lombardy (or Milan) was the most valuable to Spain in the 17th century because of its strategic importance, linking Spain with Austria and through Franche Comte, with Flanders. It served as a barrier to French invasion of Italy. Naples and Sicily were not scenes of foreign invasion as was the north of Italy.

12.2.1 *Independent Italian States*

The Duchy of Tuscany had lost its earlier eminence in art and literature. The prosperous Republic of Genoa did not influence European affairs. The Republic of Venetia no longer challenged Turkey in the eastern Mediterranean.

12.2.2 *Savoy*

Savoy was the only state with a native Italian dynasty. In the early 16th century, Savoy was a battleground between the French and the Spanish.

Emmanuel Philibert, Duke of Savoy (1553 – 80), was rewarded by the Holy Roman Emperor with the restoration of independence of Savoy. He built Savoy as a modern state.

Charles Emmanuel I (1580 – 1630), maintained his independence by playing off France diplomatically against Spain and vice versa. Neither country could permit the other to gain a foothold in strategic Savoy, so Savoy remained independent.

Victor Amadeus (1630 – 37), married Marie Christine, Louis XIII's sister, thus increasing French influence in Savoy. Charles Emmanuel II (1637 – 75) was similarly dominated by France.

Victor Amadeus II (1675 – 1731), championed the Protestant Vaudois against Louis XIV. He joined William of Orange and the League of Augsburg against France. France defeated Savoy and forced Savoy to change sides. Nevertheless, the Peace of Ryswick confirmed Savoy's independence and left Savoy the leading Italian state and an important entity in the balance of power.

In 1713 Victor Amadeus was awarded Sicily and in 1720 exchanged Sicily to Austria for the island of Sardinia. henceforth he was known as the King of Sardinia.

Charles Emmanuel III (1731 – 1773) joined France and Spain in the War of the Polish Succession in an unsuccessful attempt to drive Austria out of Italy. Savoy sided with Austria in the War of the Austrian Succession and received part of Milan as a reward.

The French Revolution and Napoleon's invasion of Austria completely changed the situation for Italy and in the 19th century Italian unification was achieved under a Sardinian king, Victor Emmanuel II.

CHAPTER 13

THE OTTOMAN TURKISH EMPIRE IN EUROPE

13.1 CHRISTIAN EUROPE VERSUS ISLAMIC MEDITERRANEAN

During the Middle Ages the Islamic Empire included Spain, North Africa, and the Middle East. Expansion of Islam into Europe was blocked by France in the West (and, after 1492, by Spain) and by the Byzantine Empire in the East. When Constantinople fell to the Ottoman Turks in 1453, Eastern Europe was open for Islamic expansion by force of arms.

Hungary and the Hapsburg Empire became the defenders of Europe. Under Suleiman the Magnificent (d. 1566) the Turks captured Belgrade and took over nearly half of Eastern Europe. Ottoman power extended from the Euphrates River to the Danube.

13.2 TURKISH DECLINE 17TH AND 18TH CENTURIES

The Sultan headed an autocratic and absolutist political system, often controlled by intrigue, murder, and arbitrary capital punishment. Most Sultans were more preoccupied with their harem than with affairs of state.

Government finance was based more on spoils of war, tribute, and sale of offices than on a sound economy. The Turkish military and bureaucracy were dependent on the training and loyalty of Christian slaves, the famous *Janissaries* and officials of the Sultan's Household.

13.3 MOHAMMED IV (1648 – 1687)

His reign was characterized by the efficient rule of an Albanian dynasty of grand viziers, the *Kiuprilis*. Thirty thousand people were executed as the Sultan and grand vizier purged all opposition to their will.

In 1683, the Turks besieged Vienna with 200,000 men for six weeks, intending to take Vienna as they had Constantinople two centuries earlier. John Sobieski, the king of Poland, with 50,000 Polish troops, went to the relief of the city and of the Hapsburg Empire. The Turks massacred 30,000 Christian prisoners and were defeated in a terrible slaughter.

13.4 MUSTAPHA II (1695 – 1703)

Austrian and Polish armies defeated the Turks again, killing 26,000 in battle and drowning 10,000. *The Treaty of Karlowitz* (1699) recognized Austrian conquests of Hungary and Transylvania. The Ottoman Empire never recovered its former power or aggressiveness.

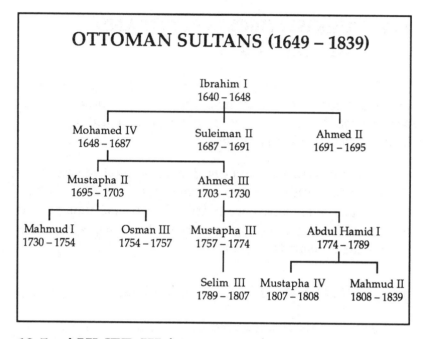

OTTOMAN SULTANS (1649 – 1839)

Ibrahim I
1640 – 1648

Mohamed IV
1648 – 1687

Suleiman II
1687 – 1691

Ahmed II
1691 – 1695

Mustapha II
1695 – 1703

Ahmed III
1703 – 1730

Mahmud I
1730 – 1754

Osman III
1754 – 1757

Mustapha III
1757 – 1774

Abdul Hamid I
1774 – 1789

Selim III
1789 – 1807

Mustapha IV
1807 – 1808

Mahmud II
1808 – 1839

13.5   AHMED III (1703 – 1730)

In 1711, the Turks attacked the Russians and forced Peter the Great to surrender and restore the Black Sea part of Azov.

In 1716, Austria destroyed 20,000 men in forcing the Turks away from Belgrade, and overran Serbia. The *Treaty of Passarowitz* (1718) ceded the rest of Hungary and the great fortress of Belgrade to Austria. The Sultan abdicated in the face of a rebellion of the Janissaries.

13.6   MAHMUD I (1730 – 1754)

Power was wielded by the chief eunuch in Mahmud's harem, Bashir, an Abyssinian slave who elevated and deposed sixteen grand viziers.

Austria and Russia coalesced to dismember the Turkish

OTTOMAN ADVANCES
INTO EASTERN EUROPE

Empire. Russia regained Azov in 1737, but Austria was defeated and gave up Belgrade in 1739.

The Janissaries disintegrated as an effective military force when the Sultan began selling the rank of Janissary to anyone willing to pay for it.

Provincial governors became more independent of the Sultan.

13.7 ABDUL HAMID I (1774 – 1789)

In the *Treaty of Kutchuk-Kainardji* (1774) Catherine the Great forced the Turks to surrender the Crimea and to recognize Russia's right to protect Eastern Orthodox Christians in the Balkans.

Russia and Austria declared war on Turkey in 1788 and Austria re-captured Belgrade in 1789.

The Ottoman Empire was no longer an important power in Europe. Competition to take over parts of Eastern Europe, especially the Balkans, was called the "Eastern Question" in European history and was a causal factor in starting World War I.

CHAPTER 14

CULTURE OF THE BAROQUE AND ROCOCO

14.1 AGE OF THE BAROQUE (1600 – 1750)

The baroque emphasized grandeur, spaciousness, unity, and the emotional impact of a work of art. The splendor of Versailles typifies the baroque in architecture: gigantic frescoes unified around the emotional impact of a single theme is baroque art; the glory of Bach's Christmas Oratorio expresses the baroque in music. Art reflects the world- and life-view (*Weltanschauung* – way of looking at the world) that is dominant in a given age. To better understand the seventeenth and eighteenth centuries, one needs to see the values, philosophy, and attitude of the age reflected in baroque art, architecture, and music. Although the baroque began in Catholic counter-reformation countries to teach in a concrete, emotional way, it soon spread to Protestant nations as well and some of the greatest baroque artists and composers were Protestant (e.g., Johann Sebastian Bach and George Frideric Handel).

14.1.1 *Baroque Architecture*

Michelangelo's work provided much of the initial inspiration for baroque architecture. A dynamic and unified treatment of all the elements of architecture combined in the baroque. Oval or elliptical plans were often used in baroque church design. Gianlorenzo Bernini (1598 – 1650) was perhaps the leading early baroque sculptor as well as an architect, and a great painter. Bernini's most famous architectural achievement was the colonnade for the piazza in front of St. Peter's Basilica in Rome. Louis XIV brought Bernini to Paris to plan a design for the completion of the palace of the Louvre, but the final design selected was that of Claude Perrault (1613 – 1688).

Louis XIV's magnificent palace at Versailles was particularly the work of Louis LeVau (1612 – 70), and Jules Mansart. The geometric design of the palace included the gardens which excel in symmetry and balance. The many fountains are also typical of the baroque.

14.1.2 *Baroque Art*

Baroque art concentrated more on broad areas of light and shadow rather than on linear arrangements as in the High Renaissance. Color was an important element because it appealed to the senses and was more true to nature. The baroque was not as concerned with clarity of detail as with the overall dynamic effect. It was designed to give a spontaneous personal experience.

Leaders in baroque painting were Annibale Carracci (1560 – 1609) from Bologna and (Michelangelo Merisi) Caravaggio (1573 – 1610) from near Milan. They are known for the concrete realism of their subjects. Their work is forceful and dramatic with sharp contrasts of light and darkness (*chiaroscuro*).

The Flemish painter Peter Paul Rubens (1577 – 1640) is one of the most famous of baroque artists. He emphasized color and sensuality.

There existed, of course, other types of painting along with the baroque. An example was the school of Italian genre painters known as *bamboccianti* who painted street scenes of Roman peasant life on a small scale.

Rembrandt Van Rijn (1606 – 69) the great Dutch painter, was so unique that he could not be considered typically baroque. Nicolas Poussin (1595 – 1665) also followed a different line of reasoning. His paintings were rationally organized to give with precision a total effect of harmony and balance; even his landscapes are orderly.

14.1.3 *Baroque Music*

A major underlying presupposition of baroque music was that the text should dominate the music rather than the music dominating the text, as formerly was done. The idea that music can depict the situation in the text and express the emotion and drama intended was a major innovation of the baroque period. Instead of writing lyrics appropriate to a musical composition, the lyrics or libretto came first and was determinative in the texture and structure of the composition. Dissonance was used freely to make the music conform to the emotion in the text. Devices of melody, rhythm, harmony, and texture all contribute to emotional effects.

The baroque was a conscious effort to express a wide range of ideas and feelings vividly in music. These were intensified by sharp contrasts in the music and a variety of moods experienced: anger, excitement, exaltation, grandeur, heroism, wonder, a contemplative mood, mystic exaltation.

Bach's "St. Matthew Passion" illustrates this with a frenzied effect of cruelty and chaos obtained by a double chorus of four voices singing, "Crucify him! Crucify Him!" The jubilant Easter Oratorio reflects the triumph of the Resurrection. Violins and violas maintain a steady progression of pizzicato chords to depict the gentle knocking of Christ in the cantata, "Behold I stand at the door and knock...."

The splendor and grandeur of baroque art and architecture was similarly expressed in baroque music. Giovannia Bargieli (1555 – 1612) pioneered in this effect when he placed four groups of instruments and choirs, each complete in itself, in the galleries and balconies of St. Mark's Cathedral in Venice. The baroque followed his lead and Babrieli laid the foundation for the modern orchestra.

The concerto involving interaction between a solo instrument and a full orchestra was an innovation of the baroque. Antonio Vivaldi (1678 – 1741) pioneered with the concerto and standardized a cycle of three movements. The major-minor key system of tonality was also developed during the baroque period.

The baroque developed a new counterpoint, different from that of the Renaissance. There was still a blending of different melodic lines, but those melodies were subordinated to the harmonic scheme. Bach was particularly successful in balancing harmony and counterpoint and melody with polyphony.

George Frideric Handel (1685 – 1759) was a master of baroque grandeur, especially in his dramatic oratorios. He brought to life in his music poetic depth and his use of the chorus profoundly affected his audiences. Handel was like a painter who was at his best with gigantic frescoes that involved his audience in the whole uplifting experience.

14.2 ROCOCO

Rococo comes from a French word meaning shell or decorative scroll. It describes a tendency towards elegance, pleasantness, and even frivolity. It is in contrast to the impressive grandeur of the baroque. It has a similar decorativeness without the emotional grandeur of the baroque. It is simpler, but not plain. The effect was more sentimental than emotional.

The leader in the Rococo movement was France, and Francois Boucher (1703 – 70) was one of the most famous French rococo painters. His paintings are elegant, delicate, innocent, and sensual all at the same time, as his paintings of Madame de Pompadour and Diana well illustrate.

Characteristics of the rococo can be found in the compositions of both Franz Josef Haydn (1732 – 1809) and Wolfgang Amadeus Mozart (1759 – 91).

"The ESSENTIALS" of HISTORY

REA's **Essentials of History** series offers a new approach to the study of history that is different from what has been available previously. Compared with conventional history outlines, the **Essentials of History** offer far more detail, with fuller explanations and interpretations of historical events and developments. Compared with voluminous historical tomes and textbooks, the **Essentials of History** offer a far more concise, less ponderous overview of each of the periods they cover.

The **Essentials of History** provide quick access to needed information, and will serve as a handy reference source at all times. The **Essentials of History** are prepared with REA's customary concern for high professional quality and student needs.

UNITED STATES HISTORY
1500 to 1789 From Colony to Republic
1789 to 1841 The Developing Nation
1841 to 1877 Westward Expansion & the Civil War
1877 to 1912 Industrialism, Foreign Expansion & the Progressive Era
1912 to 1941 World War I, the Depression & the New Deal
America since 1941: Emergence as a World Power

WORLD HISTORY
Ancient History (4,500BC to 500AD) The Emergence of Western Civilization
Medieval History (500 to 1450AD) The Middle Ages

EUROPEAN HISTORY
1450 to 1648 The Renaissance, Reformation & Wars of Religion
1648 to 1789 Bourbon, Baroque & the Enlightenment
1789 to 1848 Revolution & the New European Order
1848 to 1914 Realism & Materialism
1914 to 1935 World War I & Europe in Crisis
Europe since 1935: From World War II to the Demise of Communism

CANADIAN HISTORY
Pre-Colonization to 1867 The Beginning of a Nation
1867 to Present The Post-Confederate Nation

*If you would like more information about any of these books,
complete the coupon below and return it to us or go to your local bookstore.*

RESEARCH & EDUCATION ASSOCIATION
61 Ethel Road W. • Piscataway, New Jersey 08854
Phone: (908) 819-8880

Please send me more information about your History Essentials Books

Name _____

Address _____

City _____ State _____ Zip _____